The Artificial Intelligence

SEO and SEM

Handbook

Learn Insider Secrets

Author : Erol Yöndem

Inhaltsverzeichnis

1. INTRODUCTION: 5

DEFINITION OF SEO AND SEM — 5
IMPORTANCE OF SEO AND SEM FOR BUSINESSES AND ORGANIZATIONS — 6
OVERVIEW OF THE MAIN PRINCIPLES AND TECHNIQUES OF SEO AND SEM — 7

2. KEYWORD RESEARCH AND ON-PAGE OPTIMIZATION: 9

THE ROLE OF KEYWORDS IN SEO AND SEM — 9
TECHNIQUES FOR FINDING AND SELECTING THE RIGHT KEYWORDS — 18
BEST PRACTICES FOR ON-PAGE OPTIMIZATION, INCLUDING TITLE TAGS, META DESCRIPTIONS, AND HEADER TAGS — 27

3. LINK BUILDING AND OFF-PAGE OPTIMIZATION 34

THE IMPORTANCE OF BACKLINKS FOR SEO AND SEM — 34
STRATEGIES FOR BUILDING HIGH-QUALITY BACKLINKS — 43
TECHNIQUES FOR IMPROVING THE QUALITY AND QUANTITY OF EXTERNAL LINKS POINTING TO YOUR WEBSITE — 55
BEST PRACTICES FOR ON-PAGE OPTIMIZATION, INCLUDING TITLE TAGS, META DESCRIPTIONS, AND HEADER TAGS — 61

4. LINK BUILDING AND OFF-PAGE OPTIMIZATION: 69

THE IMPORTANCE OF BACKLINKS FOR SEO AND SEM — 69
STRATEGIES FOR BUILDING HIGH-QUALITY BACKLINKS — 75
TECHNIQUES FOR IMPROVING THE QUALITY AND QUANTITY OF EXTERNAL LINKS POINTING TO YOUR WEBSITE — 86

5. LOCAL SEO AND MAPS OPTIMIZATION: 96

The role of local SEO in attracting customers from a specific geographic area   96
Techniques for optimizing your website and online presence for local search results   105
Best practices for optimizing your business listing on Google Maps   110

6. TECHNICAL SEO: 113

The importance of technical SEO for the overall performance and visibility of your website   113

Common technical issues that can impact your SEO and how to fix them   115

Techniques for improving the crawlability, indexability, and loading speed of your website   119

7. PAID SEARCH AND PPC ADVERTISING: 121

Introduction to paid search and PPC advertising   121
Setting up and managing a PPC campaign   123
Tips for optimizing your ad copy, targeting, and budget   136

8. MEASURING AND ANALYZING YOUR SEO AND SEM RESULTS: 137

Importance of tracking and measuring your SEO and SEM efforts   137
Tools and techniques for analyzing your website traffic and search engine rankings   139
Best practices for using data to inform and improve your SEO and SEM strategies   141

9. ADVANCED SEO AND SEM STRATEGIES: 143

TIPS FOR STAYING UP-TO-DATE WITH THE LATEST SEO AND SEM TRENDS AND BEST PRACTICES 143
STRATEGIES FOR BUILDING AND MAINTAINING A LONG-TERM SEO AND SEM PLAN 152

10. CONCLUSION: 155

RECAP OF THE MAIN PRINCIPLES AND TECHNIQUES OF SEO AND SEM 155
IMPORTANCE OF ONGOING LEARNING AND OPTIMIZATION FOR SUCCESSFUL SEO AND SEM 156
FUTURE OUTLOOK FOR THE FIELD OF SEO AND SEM. 157

1.Introduction:

Definition of SEO and SEM

SEO (Search Engine Optimization) is the process of improving the visibility and ranking of a website or webpage in search engine results pages (SERPs). This is typically done through a combination of on-page optimization (making changes to the website itself) and off-page optimization (building high-quality backlinks from other websites). The goal of SEO is to increase the quantity and quality of organic (non-paid) traffic to a website, making it more visible and attractive to potential customers.

SEM (Search Engine Marketing) is the practice of promoting a website or product through paid advertising on search engines. This can include pay-per-click (PPC) advertising, where advertisers pay a fee each time their ad is clicked, and search engine optimization (SEO) services, which help improve the visibility and ranking of a website in search results. SEM is a form of online marketing that can be used to drive traffic and sales to a website by placing it in front of relevant users who are searching for specific keywords or phrases.

In summary, SEO is focused on improving the visibility and ranking of a website in organic search results, while SEM is concerned with promoting a website or product through paid advertising on search engines. Both SEO and SEM can be used to increase the online presence and visibility of a business or organization, but they use different tactics and strategies to achieve this goal.

Importance of SEO and SEM for businesses and organizations

The importance of SEO and SEM for businesses and organizations can't be overstated. In today's digital age, consumers rely heavily on search engines to find information, products, and services, making it essential for businesses and organizations to have a strong online presence and to be easily discoverable by potential customers.

SEO and SEM can help businesses and organizations in the following ways:

1. Increase visibility and traffic: By optimizing their website and online presence for search engines, businesses and organizations can increase their visibility in search results, leading to more traffic to their website. This can lead to increased brand awareness and sales.

2. Improve customer acquisition: SEO and SEM can help businesses and organizations reach their target audience by targeting specific keywords and phrases that are relevant to their products or services. This can lead to more qualified leads and conversions.

3. Boost credibility and trust: A strong online presence and high search engine ranking can improve the credibility and trustworthiness of a business or organization in the eyes of potential customers.

4. Stay competitive: In today's digital landscape, it's important for businesses and organizations to stay competitive and to be visible to potential customers.

SEO and SEM can help them achieve this by improving their online visibility and ranking.

Overall, SEO and SEM are crucial for businesses and organizations that want to attract and retain customers, stay competitive, and grow their online presence.

Overview of the main principles and techniques of SEO and SEM

1. Keyword research: One of the fundamental principles of SEO and SEM is keyword research, which involves identifying the terms and phrases that potential customers are using to search for products, services, and information. Keyword research helps businesses and organizations understand the needs and interests of their target audience and optimize their website and online presence accordingly.

2. On-page optimization: On-page optimization involves making changes to the content and structure of a website to make it more attractive to search engines and users. This can include optimizing title tags, meta descriptions, header tags, and the content itself to include relevant keywords and phrases.

3. Link building: Link building is the process of acquiring high-quality backlinks from other websites. Backlinks act as a vote of confidence for a website and can improve its credibility and ranking in search results.

4. Technical SEO: Technical SEO involves optimizing the technical aspects of a website to improve its crawlability, indexability, and loading speed. This can include

improving the website's sitemap, fixing broken links, and optimizing images and other media files.

5. Paid search and PPC advertising: SEM involves promoting a website or product through paid advertising on search engines. This can include pay-per-click (PPC) advertising, where businesses and organizations pay a fee each time their ad is clicked.

6. Measuring and analyzing results: It's important for businesses and organizations to track and measure the results of their SEO and SEM efforts to understand what's working and what's not. This can be done through tools such as Google Analytics and by tracking key performance indicators (KPIs) such as website traffic, search engine rankings, and conversions.

7. Advanced SEO and SEM strategies: As businesses and organizations become more experienced with SEO and SEM, they can start implementing more advanced strategies to further improve their online visibility and ranking. This can include things like schema markup, voice search optimization, and structured data.

Overall, these are the main principles and techniques that businesses and organizations can use to improve their online presence and visibility through SEO and SEM.

2. Keyword Research and On-Page Optimization:

The role of keywords in SEO and SEM

Keywords play a crucial role in both SEO and SEM. They are the terms and phrases that people use to search for information, products, and services online. By understanding and targeting the right keywords, businesses and organizations can improve their visibility and ranking in search results and reach their target audience more effectively.

Here are a few ways that keywords are used in SEO and SEM:

1. On-page optimization: Keywords are used in on-page optimization to signal to search engines the topic and relevance of a website or webpage. This can include incorporating keywords into the title tags, meta descriptions, header tags, and the content itself.

Sample:

Let's say that a website sells handmade jewelry and wants to optimize its pages for the keyword "handmade jewelry." Here are a few ways that the website could incorporate the keyword into its on-page optimization:

- Title tag: The title tag is the text that appears in the tab of a browser and is used to describe the content of a webpage. For example, the website could use the title tag "Handmade Jewelry | Unique and Affordable Gifts" to signal to search engines that the webpage is relevant to the keyword "handmade jewelry."

- Meta description: The meta description is the brief summary of a webpage that appears in search results. For example, the website could use the meta description "Shop our selection of handmade jewelry, perfect for any occasion. Our unique and affordable pieces make great gifts for friends and loved ones." to include the keyword "handmade jewelry" and provide additional context to search engines about the content of the webpage.

- Header tags: Header tags are used to organize and structure the content of a webpage. For example, the website could use the header tag "Find the Perfect Handmade Jewelry Piece" to signal to search engines that the content of the webpage is relevant to the keyword "handmade jewelry."

- Content: The website could also include the keyword "handmade jewelry" in the content of the webpage, such as in the body of the page or in the product descriptions. This helps signal to search engines that the webpage is relevant to the keyword and provides additional context to users about the content of the page.

By incorporating the keyword "handmade jewelry" into the title tag, meta description, header tags, and content, the website can optimize its pages for the keyword and signal to search engines the topic and relevance of the webpage.

Free Tools:

- Google Keyword Planner: This tool, which is part of Google Ads, can help a website research and select the most effective keywords for its content. It provides data on search volume, competition, and other metrics that can help a website understand which keywords are most relevant and effective. Website: https://ads.google.com/home/tools/keyword-planner/

- SEMrush: This tool provides data on keywords, as well as information on a website's traffic, ranking, and competitors. It can help a website understand which keywords are driving traffic to its website and identify opportunities to optimize its content for specific keywords. Website: https://www.semrush.com/

- Yoast SEO: This is a plugin for WordPress websites that helps optimize a website's pages for specific keywords. It provides suggestions for improving the title tag, meta description, and content of a webpage to ensure that it is optimized for a specific keyword. Website: https://yoast.com/

By using tools such as Google Keyword Planner, SEMrush, and Yoast SEO, a website can research and select the most effective keywords for its content and optimize its pages for those keywords to improve its ranking in search results.

2. PPC advertising: In PPC advertising, businesses and organizations bid on specific keywords and pay a fee each time their ad is clicked. Keywords are used to match ads with relevant searches and to help determine the ad's placement in search results.

Sample:

Let's say that a local coffee shop wants to promote its new line of organic fair trade coffee beans through PPC advertising. The coffee shop could set up a campaign on Google Ads (formerly known as Google AdWords) and bid on keywords related to "organic fair trade coffee beans."

When a user searches for one of these keywords, the coffee shop's ad may appear in the search results. The ad's placement and visibility in the search results will depend on the coffee shop's bid amount and the relevance and quality of the ad. If a user clicks on the ad, the coffee shop will pay the amount it bid for the keyword.

For example, the coffee shop could bid on the keyword "organic fair trade coffee beans" and set up an ad with the headline "Try Our Delicious Organic Fair Trade Coffee Beans – Freshly Roasted and Delivered to Your Door!" When a user searches for "organic fair trade coffee beans," the coffee shop's ad may appear in the search results, and if the user clicks on the ad, the coffee shop will pay the amount it bid for the keyword.

By bidding on relevant keywords and creating an engaging ad, the coffee shop can use PPC advertising to reach its target audience and drive traffic to its website.

Free Tools:

Here are some free tools that the coffee shop could use to set up a PPC campaign and bid on keywords:

- Google Ads: Google Ads is a pay-per-click (PPC) advertising platform that allows businesses to create and run ads on Google and its advertising network. The coffee shop could set up a campaign on Google Ads and bid on keywords related to "organic fair trade coffee beans" to reach its target audience and drive traffic to its website. Website: https://ads.google.com/home/

- Bing Ads: Bing Ads is a PPC advertising platform that allows businesses to create and run ads on Bing and its advertising network. The coffee shop could set up a campaign on Bing Ads and bid on keywords related to "organic fair trade coffee beans" to reach its target audience and drive traffic to its website. Website: https://www.bingads.microsoft.com/

- Facebook Ads: Facebook Ads is a PPC advertising platform that allows businesses to create and run ads on Facebook and its advertising network. The coffee shop could set up a campaign on Facebook Ads and bid on keywords related to "organic fair trade coffee beans" to reach its target audience and drive traffic to its website. Website: https://www.facebook.com/business/ads

By using tools such as Google Ads, Bing Ads, and Facebook Ads, the coffee shop can set up a PPC campaign and bid on relevant keywords to reach its target audience and drive traffic to its website.

3. Targeting the right audience: By understanding the keywords that their target audience is using to search for products or services, businesses and organizations can tailor their marketing efforts to reach the right people at the right time.

Sample:

Let's say that a clothing company wants to promote its new line of sustainable fashion products. By understanding the keywords that their target audience is using to search for sustainable fashion products, the company can tailor its marketing efforts to reach the right people at the right time.

For example, the company could conduct keyword research and find that the keywords "sustainable fashion," "ethically made clothing," and "sustainable fashion brands" are popular among their target audience. By targeting these keywords in their marketing efforts, such as in their website content, social media posts, and PPC advertising, the company can reach potential customers who are interested in sustainable fashion and are more likely to make a purchase.

By understanding the keywords that their target audience is using to search for products or services, businesses and organizations can tailor their marketing efforts to reach the right people at the right time and increase their chances of making a sale.

Free Tools:

Here are some free tools that a business or organization can use to track the performance of specific keywords and understand which tactics are working:

- Google Analytics: Google Analytics is a free tool that provides data on website traffic, including the keywords that drive traffic to a website. By analyzing this data, businesses and organizations can understand which keywords are driving the most traffic, conversions, and can adjust their marketing efforts accordingly. Website: https://www.google.com/analytics/

- Google Search Console: Google Search Console is a free tool that provides data on how a website is performing in search results, including the keywords that are driving traffic to the website. By analyzing this data, businesses and organizations can understand which keywords are performing well and which ones need improvement. Website: https://search.google.com/search-console

- Ahrefs: Ahrefs is a paid tool that provides data on the traffic and ranking of a website, as well as the keywords that are driving traffic to the website. Ahrefs also provides information on the quality and relevance of backlinks, which can impact a website's ranking in search results. Website: https://www.ahrefs.com/

Overall, tracking the performance of specific keywords is an important part of SEO and SEM and can help businesses and organizations understand which tactics are working and which ones need improvement. By using tools such as Google Analytics, Google Search Console, and Ahrefs, businesses and organizations can track the performance of specific keywords and make informed decisions about their marketing efforts.

4. Tracking progress: Keywords can also be used to track the success of SEO and SEM efforts. By analyzing the performance of specific keywords, businesses and organizations can understand which tactics are working and which ones need improvement.

Sample:

Let's say that a small business wants to track the success of its SEO and SEM efforts for the keyword "handmade jewelry." The business could use a tool such as Google Analytics to track the performance of the keyword over time.

Google Analytics provides a wealth of data on the performance of specific keywords, including the number of clicks, impressions, and conversions generated by the keyword. By analyzing this data, the business can understand how well its website is performing for the keyword "handmade jewelry" and whether its SEO and SEM efforts are effective.

For example, if the business sees a spike in traffic and conversions for the keyword "handmade jewelry," it could conclude that its SEO and SEM efforts are working well and that the keyword is a strong performer. On the other hand, if the business sees a decline in traffic and conversions for the keyword, it could conclude that its SEO and SEM efforts are not working as well and may need to be revised.

By analyzing the performance of specific keywords, businesses and organizations can understand which tactics are working, which ones need improvement, and make adjustments to their SEO and SEM strategies accordingly.

Free Tools:

Here is a list of some other free tools that businesses and organizations can use to track the success of their SEO and SEM efforts:

- Google Analytics: As mentioned in the sample, Google Analytics is a tool that provides a wealth of data on the performance of specific keywords, including the number of clicks, impressions, and conversions generated by the keyword. Google Analytics also provides data on website traffic, user behavior, and other metrics that can help businesses and organizations understand the success of their SEO and SEM efforts. Website: https://www.google.com/analytics/

- SEMrush: SEMrush is a tool that provides data on keyword performance, traffic, and other metrics. SEMrush also offers a keyword research tool and a site audit tool that can help businesses and organizations identify and fix issues with their website that may be impacting their ranking in search results. Website: https://www.semrush.com/

- MOZ: MOZ is a tool that provides data on keyword performance, backlinks, and other metrics. MOZ also offers a keyword research tool and a site audit tool that can help businesses and organizations improve their ranking in search results. Website: https://moz.com/

- Ahrefs: Ahrefs is a tool that provides data on keyword performance, backlinks, and other metrics. Ahrefs also offers a keyword research tool and a site audit tool that can help businesses and organizations improve their ranking in search results. Website: https://www.ahrefs.com/

By using tools such as Google Analytics, SEMrush, MOZ, and Ahrefs, businesses and organizations can track the success of their SEO and SEM efforts and make adjustments to their strategies accordingly. These tools can provide valuable insights into the performance of specific keywords and help businesses and organizations understand which tactics are working and which ones need improvement.

Overall, keywords are an essential component of SEO and SEM and play a crucial role in helping businesses and organizations reach their target audience and improve their online visibility and ranking.

Techniques for finding and selecting the right keywords

There are several techniques that businesses and organizations can use to find and select the right keywords for their SEO and SEM efforts:

1. Keyword research tools: There are several tools available that can help businesses and organizations find and analyze keywords, such as Google's Keyword

Planner, Ahrefs, and SEMrush. These tools provide data on search volume, competition, and other metrics that can help businesses and organizations select the most relevant and effective keywords.

Sample:

Let's say that a small business wants to optimize its website for the keyword "handmade jewelry." The business could use a keyword research tool such as Google's Keyword Planner to find and analyze keywords related to "handmade jewelry."

To use the Keyword Planner, the business would enter the keyword "handmade jewelry" and set its target location and language. The Keyword Planner would then return a list of related keywords and provide data on their search volume, competition level, and cost-per-click (CPC) if the business were to bid on the keyword in a PPC campaign.

For example, the Keyword Planner might return the following data for the keyword "handmade jewelry":

- Search volume: 1,000 searches per month
- Competition: Low
- CPC: $1.50

Based on this data, the business could conclude that the keyword "handmade jewelry" has a moderate search volume, low competition, and a relatively low CPC, making it a potentially effective keyword to target in its SEO and SEM efforts.

By using a keyword research tool such as Google's Keyword Planner, businesses and organizations can find and analyze relevant keywords and select the most effective ones for their SEO and SEM efforts.

Free Tools:

Here are some additional free keyword research tools with their websites:

- Ubersuggest: https://www.ubersuggest.com/
- Keywordtool.io: https://keywordtool.io/
- KWFinder: https://www.kwfinder.com/
- SEMrush: https://www.semrush.com/

Each of these tools offers different features and capabilities, so it's a good idea to try out a few different ones to see which one works best for your needs. Some of these tools may have limited functionality in their free versions, but they still provide valuable insights and can be a useful resource for businesses and organizations looking to find and analyze keywords.

2. Customer feedback and reviews: Businesses and organizations can also gather insights into the keywords that their customers are using by analyzing customer feedback and reviews. By looking at the language and terms that customers use to describe their products or services, businesses and organizations can identify keywords that are relevant to their target audience.

Sample:

Let's say that a clothing company wants to optimize its website for the keyword "sustainable fashion." One way the company can gather insights into the keywords that their customers are using is by analyzing customer feedback and reviews.

The company could start by collecting customer feedback and reviews from various sources, such as its website, social media channels, and review websites. By looking at the language and terms that customers use to describe the company's products and services, the company can identify keywords that are relevant to its target audience.

For example, the company might find that customers frequently use the terms "ethically made," "sustainable materials," and "conscious fashion" when describing the company's products. By incorporating these keywords into its website content, the company can optimize its pages for the keywords and signal to search engines the relevance and topic of its content.

By analyzing customer feedback and reviews, businesses and organizations can identify keywords that are relevant to their target audience and optimize their website and online presence accordingly.

Free Tools:
Here are some free tools that a business can use to gather insights into the keywords that their customers are using:

- Google Analytics: Google Analytics is a free tool that provides data on the traffic and behavior of a website.

By analyzing the keywords that users are searching for on a website, businesses and organizations can identify keywords that are relevant to their target audience. Google Analytics also provides data on the demographics, interests, and location of a website's users, which can be helpful for targeting the right audience. Website: https://www.google.com/analytics/

- Google My Business: Google My Business is a free tool that allows businesses and organizations to manage their online presence on Google, including their Google Maps listing and Google search results. By analyzing the keywords that users are searching for to find a business, businesses and organizations can identify keywords that are relevant to their target audience. Website: https://www.google.com/business/

- Social media analytics: Many social media platforms, such as Facebook, Twitter, and Instagram, offer analytics tools that can provide insights into the keywords that users are using to find and engage with a business. By analyzing this data, businesses and organizations can identify keywords that are relevant to their target audience and optimize their social media content accordingly.

By using tools such as Google Analytics, Google My Business, and social media analytics, businesses and organizations can gather insights into the keywords that their customers are using and optimize their website and online presence accordingly.

3. Competitor analysis: Analyzing the keywords that competitors are using can also provide valuable insights into the most effective keywords for a particular industry or market. By examining the keywords that competitors are ranking for, businesses and organizations can identify gaps in their own keyword strategy and target similar keywords to improve their own ranking.

Sample:

Let's say that a small business wants to optimize its website for the keyword "handmade jewelry." One way the business can gather insights into the keywords that are effective in its industry is by analyzing the keywords that its competitors are using.

To do this, the business could use a tool such as Ahrefs or SEMrush to examine the keywords that its competitors are ranking for in search results. These tools provide data on the keywords that a website is ranking for, as well as their search volume and ranking position.

By analyzing the keywords that its competitors are ranking for, the business can identify gaps in its own keyword strategy and target similar keywords to improve its own ranking. For example, the business might find that its competitors are ranking for the keywords "unique handmade jewelry" and "handcrafted jewelry," which could be good keywords for the business to target as well.

By analyzing the keywords that competitors are using, businesses and organizations can identify gaps in their own keyword strategy and target similar keywords to improve their own ranking and online visibility.

Free Tools:

Here are some free tools that businesses and organizations can use to analyze the keywords that their competitors are using:

- Ahrefs: Ahrefs is a tool that provides data on the keywords that a website is ranking for, as well as their search volume and ranking position. It also provides data on the backlinks that a website has and the traffic it is receiving. Ahrefs offers a free trial of its tool, which can be used to analyze the keywords that competitors are using. https://www.ahrefs.com/

- SEMrush: SEMrush is a tool that provides data on the keywords that a website is ranking for, as well as their search volume and ranking position. It also provides data on the traffic that a website is receiving and the backlinks it has. SEMrush offers a limited free version of its tool, which can be used to analyze the keywords that competitors are using. https://www.semrush.com/

- Google Keyword Planner: Google Keyword Planner is a tool that provides data on the search volume and competition level of specific keywords. It can be used to identify potential keywords to target in SEO and SEM efforts and to see how those keywords are performing. https://ads.google.com/home/tools/keyword-planner/

- Ubersuggest: Ubersuggest is a tool that provides data on the keywords that a website is ranking for, as well as their search volume and ranking position. It also provides suggestions for related keywords that a business or organization could target in its SEO and SEM efforts. Ubersuggest offers a free version of its tool, which can be used to analyze the keywords that competitors are using. https://www.ubersuggest.com/

By using these tools, businesses and organizations can analyze the keywords that their competitors are using and identify gaps in their own keyword strategy. By targeting similar keywords, businesses and organizations can improve their ranking and online visibility in search results.

4. Long-tail keywords: In addition to targeting more general and competitive keywords, businesses and organizations can also consider targeting long-tail keywords, which are more specific and less competitive. Long-tail keywords can be more effective at driving qualified traffic and conversions because they are more targeted and relevant to the business or organization's products or services.

Sample:

Let's say that a small business sells handmade jewelry and wants to optimize its website for the keyword "handmade jewelry." While this is a broad and competitive keyword, the business could also consider targeting long-tail keywords that are more specific and less competitive.

One way the business could find long-tail keywords is by using a keyword research tool such as Google's Keyword Planner or Ahrefs. These tools provide data on the search volume and competition level of specific keywords, which can help businesses and organizations identify long-tail keywords that are relevant to their products or services.

For example, the business might find that the long-tail keyword "handmade silver bracelet" has a lower search volume and competition level compared to the general keyword "handmade jewelry." By targeting this long-tail keyword in its website content and PPC campaigns, the business can reach a more targeted and qualified audience and potentially drive more conversions.

Overall, long-tail keywords can be an effective way for businesses and organizations to drive qualified traffic and conversions by targeting specific and relevant keywords that are less competitive.

By using these techniques, businesses and organizations can find and select the right keywords to optimize their website and online presence for search engines and reach their target audience more effectively.

Free Tools:

Here are some additional free keyword research tools that businesses and organizations can use to find long-tail keywords:

- Ubersuggest: Ubersuggest is a keyword research tool that provides data on the search volume and competition level of specific keywords. It also offers suggestions for related keywords and phrases. Ubersuggest can be accessed for free at https://www.ubersuggest.com/

- Keywordtool.io: Keywordtool.io is a keyword research tool that generates suggestions for keywords based on a given seed keyword. It provides data on the search volume and competition level of specific keywords, as well as suggestions for related keywords and phrases. Keywordtool.io can be accessed for free at https://keywordtool.io/

- Answer the Public: Answer the Public is a keyword research tool that generates suggestions for keywords based on a given seed keyword. It provides data on the search volume and competition level of specific keywords, as well as suggestions for related keywords and phrases. Answer the Public can be accessed for free at https://answerthepublic.com/

Overall, these keyword research tools can be useful for businesses and organizations looking to find long-tail keywords that are specific and relevant to their products or services. By using these tools, businesses and organizations can identify long-tail keywords that have a lower search volume and competition level and can be used to optimize their website and online presence for search engines and reach their target audience more effectively.

Best practices for on-page optimization, including title tags, meta descriptions, and header tags

On-page optimization refers to the practice of optimizing individual web pages in order to rank higher and earn more relevant traffic in search engines. There are several best practices for on-page optimization that businesses and organizations can follow, including:

1. Title tags: Title tags are the text that appears in the tab of a browser and are used to describe the content of a webpage. Title tags should be descriptive and concise, and should include the primary keyword for the webpage. It's also a good idea to include the brand name in the title tag to help establish trust and credibility.

Sample:

Let's say that a small business sells handmade jewelry and wants to optimize its website for the keyword "handmade jewelry." One way the business can optimize its website is by using descriptive and concise title tags that include the primary keyword "handmade jewelry."

For example, the business could use the following title tag for its homepage: "Handmade Jewelry | Unique and Affordable Gifts | [Brand Name]"

This title tag includes the primary keyword "handmade jewelry" and provides additional context about the content of the webpage. It also includes the brand name, which helps establish trust and credibility with users.

By using descriptive and concise title tags that include the primary keyword and the brand name, businesses and organizations can optimize their website and signal to search engines the topic and relevance of their webpages.

Free Tools:
Here are some free tools that businesses and organizations can use to optimize their website, including their website links:

- Google Search Console: https://search.google.com/search-console Google Search Console is a free tool that businesses and organizations can use to optimize their website for search engines. It provides data on how a website is performing in search results, including the keywords that are driving traffic to the website and any technical issues that may be impacting its ranking.

- Ahrefs: https://www.ahrefs.com/ Ahrefs is a paid tool that offers a limited number of free searches per day. It provides data on the performance of a website in search results, including the quality and relevance of its backlinks, as well as information on the traffic and ranking of the website.

- SEMrush: https://www.semrush.com/ SEMrush is a paid tool that offers a limited number of free searches per day. It provides data on the performance of a website in search results, including the keywords that are driving traffic to the website and the competitors that are ranking for those keywords.

Overall, these tools can be useful for businesses and organizations looking to optimize their website for search engines. By using data from these tools, businesses and organizations can identify opportunities to improve their website's ranking in search results and make informed decisions about their SEO and SEM strategy.

2. Meta descriptions: Meta descriptions are the brief summary of a webpage that appears in search results. Meta descriptions should be informative and persuasive, and should include the primary keyword for the webpage. It's also a good idea to include a call-to-action (such as "Learn more" or "Shop now") in the meta description to encourage users to click on the webpage.

Sample:

Let's say that a small business sells handmade jewelry and wants to optimize its website for the keyword "handmade jewelry." One way the business can optimize its website is by using informative and persuasive meta descriptions that include the primary keyword "handmade jewelry" and a call-to-action.

For example, the business could use the following meta description for its homepage: "Shop our selection of unique handmade jewelry at affordable prices. From statement rings to delicate pendants, find the perfect gift for yourself or a loved one. Learn more and shop now."

This meta description includes the primary keyword "handmade jewelry" and provides information about the content of the webpage. It also includes a call-to-action, "Learn more and shop now," which encourages users to click on the webpage.

By using informative and persuasive meta descriptions that include the primary keyword and a call-to-action, businesses and organizations can optimize their website and encourage users to click on their webpages.

Free Tools:

Here are some free tools that businesses and organizations can use to optimize their website, including their meta descriptions:

- Google Search Console: https://search.google.com/search-console Google Search Console is a free tool offered by Google that allows businesses and organizations to track their website's performance in search results and identify any issues that may be affecting their ranking. It also provides data on the keywords that users are searching for to find the website, which can help businesses and organizations optimize their meta descriptions.

- Yoast SEO: https://yoast.com/ Yoast SEO is a free plugin for WordPress websites that helps businesses and organizations optimize their website for search engines. It includes a feature that analyzes the meta descriptions of webpages and provides recommendations for improvement.

- SEMrush: https://www.semrush.com/ SEMrush is a paid tool, but it offers a limited number of free searches per day. It provides data on the keywords that a website is ranking for and offers suggestions for improving the website's ranking, including optimizing meta descriptions.

By using tools such as Google Search Console, Yoast SEO, and SEMrush, businesses and organizations can optimize their website, including their meta descriptions, and improve their ranking in search results.

3. Header tags: Header tags are used to organize and structure the content of a webpage. It's a good idea to use header tags to break up the content into sections and subheadings, and to include the primary keyword for the webpage in at least one header tag.

Sample:

Let's say that a small business sells handmade jewelry and wants to optimize its website for the keyword "handmade jewelry." One way the business can optimize its website is by using header tags to organize and structure the content of its webpages and include the primary keyword "handmade jewelry."

For example, the business could use the following header tags on its homepage:

- H1: "Handmade Jewelry – Unique and Affordable Gifts"
- H2: "Statement Rings"
- H2: " Delicate Pendants"
- H2: " Handcrafted Earrings"

By using header tags to break up the content into sections and subheadings and by including the primary keyword "handmade jewelry" in at least one header tag, the business can signal to search engines the topic and relevance of its content and make it more easily navigable for users.

Overall, header tags are an important component of on-page optimization and should be used to organize and structure the content of a webpage and signal to search engines the topic and relevance of the content.

Overall, title tags, meta descriptions, and header tags are important components of on-page optimization and should be carefully crafted to signal to search engines the topic and relevance of a webpage and to encourage users to click on the webpage.

Free Tools:

Here are some free tools that businesses and organizations can use to optimize their websites and include header tags:

- Yoast SEO: Yoast SEO is a plugin for WordPress websites that helps businesses and organizations optimize their content for search engines. Yoast SEO includes a feature that allows businesses and organizations to easily add header tags to their webpages and ensure that they are being used correctly. Website: https://yoast.com/

- SEMrush: SEMrush is a tool that provides businesses and organizations with data on their website's SEO and helps them optimize their content for search engines. SEMrush includes a feature called On Page SEO Checker that analyzes the use of header tags on a webpage and provides recommendations for improvement. Website: https://www.semrush.com/

- Moz: Moz is a tool that provides businesses and organizations with data on their website's SEO and helps them optimize their content for search engines. Moz includes a feature called On Page Grader that analyzes the use of header tags on a webpage and provides recommendations for improvement. Website: https://moz.com/

Overall, these tools can be helpful for businesses and organizations that want to optimize their websites and use header tags effectively. By using these tools, businesses and organizations can ensure that their header tags are being used correctly and signal to search engines the topic and relevance of their content.

3. Link Building and Off-Page Optimization

The importance of backlinks for SEO and SEM

Backlinks, also known as inbound links or external links, are links from other websites that point to a specific webpage. Backlinks are important for SEO and SEM because they signal to search engines the importance and credibility of a webpage. In general, the more backlinks a webpage has from high-quality and relevant websites, the higher it will rank in search results.

There are several ways that businesses and organizations can use backlinks to improve their SEO and SEM efforts:

1. Link building: One way to acquire backlinks is through link building, which involves actively seeking out and obtaining links from other websites. This can be done through a variety of methods, such as guest blogging, broken link building, and content syndication.

Sample:

Let's say that a small business sells handmade jewelry and wants to improve its ranking in search results for the keyword "handmade jewelry." One way the business can acquire backlinks is through link building.

There are several link building methods that the business could use, such as:

- Guest blogging: The business could write guest blog posts for other websites in its industry and include a link back to its own website in the blog post. This can be an effective way to build relationships with other websites and acquire backlinks.

- Broken link building: The business could also find broken links on other websites and offer to replace them with a link to its own website. This can be a win-win situation, as it helps the other website fix a broken link and provides the business with a backlink.

- Content syndication: The business could also syndicate its content on other websites and include a link back to its own website. This can help the business reach a wider audience and acquire backlinks at the same time.

Overall, link building is an effective way for businesses and organizations to acquire backlinks and improve their ranking in search results. By using methods such as guest blogging, broken link building, and content syndication, businesses and organizations can build relationships with other websites and acquire valuable backlinks.

Free Tools:

Here are some free tools that businesses and organizations can use to assist with link building efforts:

- Moz Link Explorer: This tool is a comprehensive link analysis tool that provides data on the quality and quantity of backlinks to a website, as well as insights into the ranking and traffic of a website. Website: https://moz.com/link-explorer

- Ahrefs: This tool is a comprehensive SEO tool that provides data on backlinks, as well as information on the traffic and ranking of a website. Ahrefs also has a link building tool that helps businesses and organizations find opportunities for link building. Website: https://www.ahrefs.com/

- SEMrush: This tool is a comprehensive marketing tool that provides data on backlinks, as well as information on the traffic and ranking of a website. SEMrush also has a link building tool that helps businesses and organizations find opportunities for link building. Website: https://www.semrush.com/

- Majestic: This tool is a comprehensive link analysis tool that provides data on the quality and quantity of backlinks to a website, as well as insights into the ranking and traffic of a website. Website: https://majestic.com/

- Linkstant: This tool is a link building tool that helps businesses and organizations find opportunities for link building. Linkstant also provides alerts when a website acquires a new backlink. Website: https://linkstant.com/

Overall, these free tools can be helpful for businesses and organizations looking to build high-quality backlinks through methods such as guest blogging, broken link building, and content syndication. By using these tools, businesses and organizations can identify opportunities for link building and track the success of their link building efforts.

2. Content marketing: Creating high-quality and informative content can also help businesses and organizations acquire backlinks naturally. By producing content that is valuable and useful to other websites, businesses and organizations can encourage other websites to link to their content, which can improve their ranking in search results.

Sample:

Let's say that a small business sells handmade jewelry and wants to improve its ranking in search results for the keyword "handmade jewelry." One way the business can acquire backlinks naturally is through content marketing.

The business could create high-quality and informative content about handmade jewelry, such as blog posts, infographics, and videos, and publish this content on its own website. By producing content that is valuable and useful to other websites, the business can encourage other websites to link to its content, which can improve its ranking in search results.

For example, the business could write a blog post about the benefits of handmade jewelry and include links to reputable sources to support its claims. This blog post could be shared on social media and other websites, and if other websites find it valuable and useful, they may choose to link to it, which would provide the business with valuable backlinks.

Trends in Content Marketing:

- Personalization: Many businesses and organizations are using personalization to create more relevant and targeted content for their audience. By using data and analytics, businesses and organizations can understand their audience's interests and needs and create content that resonates with them.

- Video content: Video content is becoming increasingly popular and is expected to make up over 80% of internet traffic in the next few years. Businesses and organizations can use video content, such as explainer videos and live streams, to engage their audience and drive traffic to their website.

- Interactive content: Interactive content, such as quizzes, polls, and games, can be an effective way to engage and retain an audience. By creating interactive content, businesses and organizations can encourage their audience to spend more time on their website and potentially share the content with others.

Overall, content marketing is a valuable strategy for businesses and organizations to acquire backlinks naturally and improve their ranking in search results. By creating high-quality and informative content and leveraging trends such as personalization, video content, and interactive content, businesses and organizations can engage their audience and drive traffic to their website.

Free Tools

Here are some free tools that businesses and organizations can use for content marketing:

- Canva: Canva is a graphic design tool that can be used to create infographics, social media posts, and other visual content. Canva offers a range of templates and design elements that can be easily customized to create professional-looking content. Website: https://www.canva.com/

- Hootsuite: Hootsuite is a social media management tool that can be used to schedule and publish social media posts and track the performance of social media campaigns. Hootsuite offers a range of features, including the ability to schedule and publish content across multiple social media platforms, and track metrics such as engagement and reach. Website: https://hootsuite.com/

- Grammarly: Grammarly is a writing assistance tool that can be used to improve the grammar, spelling, and style of written content. Grammarly offers a range of features, including grammar and spelling checks, style suggestions, and plagiarism detection. Website: https://www.grammarly.com/

- Buzzsumo: Buzzsumo is a content marketing tool that can be used to track the performance of content on social media and identify trends and influencers in a particular industry. Buzzsumo offers a range of features, including the ability to track the performance of content on social media, identify influencers in a particular industry, and analyze the content of competitors. Website: https://buzzsumo.com/

Overall, these tools can be useful for businesses and organizations looking to create and promote high-quality and informative content as part of their content marketing efforts. By leveraging these tools, businesses and organizations can create professional-looking content, schedule and publish social media posts, improve the quality of their written content, and track the performance of their content on social media.

3. Social media: Social media platforms such as Facebook, Twitter, and LinkedIn can also be used to promote content and acquire backlinks. By sharing content on social media and engaging with followers, businesses and organizations can drive traffic to their website and potentially acquire backlinks.

Overall, backlinks are an important factor in SEO and SEM and can help improve the ranking and visibility of a webpage in search results.

Sample:

Let's say that a small business sells handmade jewelry and wants to improve its ranking in search results for the keyword "handmade jewelry." One way the business can acquire backlinks is through content marketing.

The business could create high-quality and informative content, such as blog posts, infographics, and videos, that is valuable and useful to other websites in its industry. By producing content that is relevant and informative, the business can encourage other websites to link to its content, which can help improve its ranking in search results.

For example, the business could create a blog post about the benefits of handmade jewelry and include information about the ethical and environmental advantages of handmade jewelry compared to mass-produced jewelry. This content could be valuable and useful to other websites in the handmade jewelry industry, and they may be more likely to link to the business's content.

Trends in content marketing include:

- Personalization: Customizing content based on the user's interests and preferences can help businesses and organizations engage with their audience more effectively.

- Video content: Video content, such as video tutorials and video ads, is becoming increasingly popular and can be an effective way to engage with an audience.
- Interactive content: Interactive content, such as quizzes and polls, can be a good way to engage with an audience and encourage them to share and link to the content.

Free Tools:

here are some free tools that businesses and organizations can use to create and promote their content marketing efforts:

- Canva: Canva is a graphic design tool that can be used to create professional-looking infographics, social media graphics, and other visual content. Website: https://www.canva.com/

- Unsplash: Unsplash is a website that provides free, high-quality photos that can be used in content marketing efforts. Website: https://unsplash.com/

- BuzzSumo: BuzzSumo is a tool that can be used to find popular content in a particular industry or topic. This can be helpful for identifying trends and ideas for content marketing efforts. Website: https://buzzsumo.com/

- Hootsuite: Hootsuite is a social media management tool that can be used to schedule and promote content on social media platforms such as Facebook, Twitter, and LinkedIn. Website: https://hootsuite.com/

- Google Analytics: Google Analytics is a free tool that can be used to track the performance of content marketing efforts and understand the effectiveness of different tactics. Website: https://www.google.com/analytics/

By using tools such as Canva, Unsplash, BuzzSumo, Hootsuite, and Google Analytics, businesses and organizations can create and promote high-quality and informative content that is valuable and useful to other websites and can help acquire backlinks and improve their ranking in search results.

Overall, content marketing is an important part of SEO and SEM and can help businesses and organizations acquire backlinks naturally by producing high-quality and informative content that is valuable and useful to other websites.

Strategies for building high-quality backlinks

1. Create high-quality and informative content: As mentioned earlier, creating high-quality and informative content can help businesses and organizations acquire backlinks naturally. By producing content that is valuable and useful to other websites, businesses and organizations can encourage other websites to link to their content.

Sample:

Let's say that a small business sells handmade jewelry and wants to improve its ranking in search results for the keyword "handmade jewelry." One way the business can acquire backlinks is by creating high-quality and informative content.

The business could create a variety of content, such as blog posts, infographics, and videos, that is valuable and useful to other websites in its industry. For example, the business could create a blog post about the benefits of handmade jewelry and include information about the ethical and environmental advantages of handmade jewelry compared to mass-produced jewelry. This content could be valuable and useful to other websites in the handmade jewelry industry, and they may be more likely to link to the business's content.

The business could also create an infographic that compares the environmental impact of handmade jewelry to mass-produced jewelry. This infographic could be shared on social media and other websites, and could encourage other websites to link to it.

By creating high-quality and informative content that is valuable and useful to other websites, businesses and organizations can acquire backlinks naturally and improve their ranking in search results.

Free Tools:

To create high-quality and informative content, the small business could use tools such as Grammarly, Hemingway, and Canva. These tools can help improve the quality and clarity of the business's content and make it more attractive to other websites.

- Grammarly is a grammar and spelling checker that can help businesses and organizations produce error-free content. Grammarly can be used to check the grammar and spelling of blog posts, infographics, and other types of content. Website: https://www.grammarly.com/

- Hemingway is a tool that helps businesses and organizations improve the readability and clarity of their content. Hemingway can be used to identify and fix long or complicated sentences, passive voice, and other writing issues that can make content difficult to understand. Website: http://www.hemingwayapp.com/

- Canva is a design tool that can be used to create professional-looking infographics and other types of visual content. Canva offers a range of templates and design elements that businesses and organizations can use to create visually appealing infographics and other types of content. Website: https://www.canva.com/

Overall, by using tools such as Grammarly, Hemingway, and Canva, businesses and organizations can create high-quality and informative content that is valuable and useful to other websites, which can help acquire backlinks naturally and improve their ranking in search results.

2. Build relationships with other websites: Building relationships with other websites in the industry can be a good way to acquire backlinks. This can be done

through methods such as guest blogging, participating in online communities and forums, and attending industry events.

Sample:

Let's say that a small business sells handmade jewelry and wants to improve its ranking in search results for the keyword "handmade jewelry." One way the business can acquire backlinks is by building relationships with other websites in its industry.

The business could engage in the following activities to build relationships with other websites and acquire backlinks:

- Guest blogging: The business could write guest blog posts for other websites in its industry and include a link back to its own website in the blog post. This can be an effective way to build relationships with other websites and acquire backlinks.

- Participating in online communities and forums: The business could participate in online communities and forums related to its industry and provide valuable insights and advice. By participating in these communities, the business can build relationships with other websites and potentially acquire backlinks.

- Attending industry events: The business could attend industry events and network with other websites in its industry. By building relationships with other websites and providing value, the business can acquire backlinks naturally.

Overall, building relationships with other websites is an important part of acquiring backlinks and can be done through methods such as guest blogging, participating in online communities and forums, and attending industry events. By building relationships with other websites and providing value, businesses and organizations can acquire valuable backlinks that can help improve their ranking in search results.

Free Tools:

Here are some free tools that can help a business monitor and track its backlinks:

- Google Search Console: Google Search Console is a free tool provided by Google that allows businesses and organizations to monitor and track their website's performance in search results. It provides data on the backlinks that a website has, as well as information on the traffic and ranking of the website. Website: https://search.google.com/search-console

- Ahrefs: Ahrefs is a tool that provides data on the quality and relevance of backlinks, as well as information on the traffic and ranking of a website. It offers a free version of its tool, although it also has paid versions with additional features. Website: https://www.ahrefs.com/

- Open Site Explorer: Open Site Explorer is a tool provided by Moz that allows businesses and organizations to monitor and track their backlinks. It provides data on the quality and relevance of backlinks, as well as information on the traffic and ranking of a website. Website: https://moz.com/researchtools/ose/

- SEMrush: SEMrush is a tool that provides data on the quality and relevance of backlinks, as well as information on the traffic and ranking of a website. It offers a free version of its tool, although it also has paid versions with additional features. Website: https://www.semrush.com/

By using these tools, businesses and organizations can monitor and track their backlinks to ensure that they are high-quality and relevant, and can take action to remove any low-quality or spammy backlinks that may be impacting their ranking in search results.

3. Use social media: Social media platforms such as Facebook, Twitter, Snapchat, tiktok and LinkedIn can be used to promote content and acquire backlinks. By sharing content on social media and engaging with followers, businesses and organizations can drive traffic to their website and potentially acquire backlinks.

Sample:

Let's say that a small business sells handmade jewelry and wants to improve its ranking in search results for the keyword "handmade jewelry." One way the business can acquire backlinks is by using social media to promote its content.

The business could create a social media strategy that includes sharing its blog posts, infographics, and videos on platforms such as Facebook, Twitter, and LinkedIn. By sharing its content on social media, the business can drive traffic to its website and potentially acquire backlinks.

The business could also engage with its followers on social media by responding to comments and messages and asking for shares or links to its content. This can help increase the reach of the business's content and potentially acquire backlinks.

The business could also consider using platforms such as Snapchat and TikTok to reach a younger audience and share its content. These platforms can be particularly effective for businesses that sell products or services that appeal to younger consumers.

Overall, using social media is an important part of SEO and SEM and can help businesses and organizations acquire backlinks by promoting their content and engaging with followers. By sharing content on social media and asking for shares or links, businesses and organizations can drive traffic to their website and potentially acquire valuable backlinks that can help improve their ranking in search results.

Free Tools:

Here are some free social media management tools that a small business could use to manage its social media presence and promote its content:

- Hootsuite: Hootsuite is a social media management tool that allows businesses to schedule and publish content across multiple social media platforms, including Facebook, Twitter, LinkedIn, and Instagram. Hootsuite also provides analytics and insights to help businesses track the performance of their social media efforts. https://hootsuite.com/

- Buffer: Buffer is another social media management tool that allows businesses to schedule and publish content across multiple social media platforms. Buffer also provides analytics and insights to help businesses track the performance of their social media efforts. https://buffer.com/

- Later: Later is a social media management tool specifically designed for businesses that want to use Instagram to promote their content. Later allows businesses to schedule and publish posts on Instagram, as well as track the performance of their Instagram account. https://www.later.com/

Overall, these social media management tools can help businesses and organizations manage their social media presence, promote their content, and track the performance of their social media efforts. By using these tools to share content on social media and engage with followers, businesses and organizations can drive traffic to their website and potentially acquire valuable backlinks that can help improve their ranking in search results.

4. Check for broken links: Finding broken links on other websites and offering to replace them with a link to your own website can be a win-win situation, as it helps the other website fix a broken link and provides you with a backlink.

Sample:

Let's say that a small business sells handmade jewelry and wants to improve its ranking in search results for the keyword "handmade jewelry." One way the business can acquire backlinks is by checking for broken links on other websites and offering to replace them with a link to its own website.

The business could use a tool such as Broken Link Checker (https://www.brokenlinkcheck.com/) to scan other websites for broken links. Once the business has identified broken links on other websites, it could reach out to the website owner and offer to replace the broken link with a link to its own website. This can be a win-win situation, as it helps the other website fix a broken link and provides the business with a backlink.

Here is an example of an email the business could send to the website owner:

"Hi,

I came across your website while searching for information about handmade jewelry and noticed that you have a broken link on your page. I own a small business that sells handmade jewelry and I thought you might be interested in replacing the broken link with a link to my website.

I believe that my website would be a valuable resource for your readers and would appreciate the opportunity to provide them with more information about handmade jewelry.

Let me know if you're interested and I would be happy to send you more information about my business.

Thank you for your consideration.

Best regards, [Business name]"

Overall, checking for broken links and offering to replace them with a link to your own website is a good way to acquire backlinks and can be done using tools such as Broken Link Checker. By helping other websites fix broken links and providing value, businesses and organizations can acquire valuable backlinks that can help improve their ranking in search results.

Free Tools:

here are some additional free tools that businesses and organizations can use to check for broken links and acquire backlinks:

- Dead Link Checker (https://www.deadlinkchecker.com/): This tool allows users to scan websites for broken links and provides a report of any broken links found.

- LinkMiner (https://linkminer.com/): This tool allows users to check for broken links on a website and provides information on the status and response code of each link.

- W3C Link Checker (https://validator.w3.org/checklink): This tool allows users to check for broken links on a website and provides information on the status and location of each link.

- LinkChecker (https://wummel.github.io/linkchecker/): This tool allows users to check for broken links on a website and provides a report of any broken links found, as well as information on the status and location of each link.

By using tools such as Dead Link Checker, LinkMiner, W3C Link Checker, and LinkChecker, businesses and organizations can easily check for broken links on other websites and offer to replace them with a link to their own website. This can be an effective way to acquire backlinks and improve the ranking of a website in search results.

5. Monitor and track backlinks: It's important to regularly monitor and track backlinks to ensure that they are high-quality and relevant. If a website has low-quality or spammy backlinks, it can negatively impact its ranking in search results.

Sample:

Let's say that a small business sells handmade jewelry and wants to improve its ranking in search results for the keyword "handmade jewelry." One way the business can ensure that its backlinks are high-quality and relevant is by regularly monitoring and tracking them.

To monitor and track backlinks, the business could use tools such as Google Search Console and Ahrefs. These tools provide data on the backlinks that a website has, including the quality and relevance of the backlinks.

For example, the business could use Google Search Console to see which websites are linking to its website and whether those links are helping or hurting its ranking in search results. If the business notices that it has a high number of low-quality or spammy backlinks, it could use the disavow tool in Google Search Console to tell Google to ignore those backlinks.

Ahrefs is another tool that can be used to monitor and track backlinks. Ahrefs provides data on the quality and relevance of backlinks, as well as information on the traffic and ranking of a website.

By regularly monitoring and tracking backlinks using tools such as Google Search Console and Ahrefs, businesses and organizations can ensure that their backlinks are high-quality and relevant and can take action to remove any low-quality or spammy backlinks that may be impacting their ranking in search results.

Free Tools:

- Google Search Console: https://search.google.com/search-console
- Ahrefs: https://www.ahrefs.com/

Both Google Search Console and Ahrefs offer free versions of their tools, although they also have paid versions with additional features.

Overall, building high-quality backlinks is an important part of SEO and SEM and can help improve the ranking and visibility of a website in search results. By creating high-quality and informative content, building relationships with other websites, using social media, checking for broken links, and monitoring and tracking backlinks, businesses and organizations can acquire valuable backlinks that can help improve their ranking in search results.

Techniques for improving the quality and quantity of external links pointing to your website

Here are some techniques that businesses and organizations can use to improve the quality and quantity of external links pointing to their website:

- Create high-quality and informative content: One way to improve the quality and quantity of external links pointing to a website is by creating high-quality and informative content that is valuable and useful to other websites. By producing content that is worth linking to, businesses and organizations can encourage other websites to link to their content and improve their ranking in search results.

Sample:

Here is a sample for the technique of creating high-quality and informative content to improve the quality and quantity of external links pointing to a website:

Let's say that a small business sells handmade jewelry and wants to improve its ranking in search results for the keyword "handmade jewelry." One way the business can improve the quality and quantity of external links pointing to its website is by creating high-quality and informative content.

To do this, the business could produce content such as blog posts, infographics, and videos that provide valuable and useful information to its target audience. For example, the business could create a blog post that provides tips on how to choose the right jewelry for different occasions, or an infographic that compares the different materials used in handmade jewelry.

By producing high-quality and informative content, the business can attract other websites to link to its content and improve its ranking in search results. The business could also share its content on social media and engage with followers to drive traffic to its website and potentially acquire backlinks.

Overall, creating high-quality and informative content is an important technique for improving the quality and quantity of external links pointing to a website and can help businesses and organizations improve their ranking in search results.

Free Tools:

Here are some free artificial intelligence (AI) tools that businesses and organizations can use to create high-quality and informative content, along with their websites:

- Grammarly: Grammarly is a free AI tool that helps businesses and organizations improve the grammar and style of their written content. It can be used to check for errors, suggest alternative word choices, and provide feedback on the readability and clarity of the content. Website: https://www.grammarly.com/

- Hemingway App: The Hemingway App is a free AI tool that helps businesses and organizations improve the readability and clarity of their written content. It can be used to identify complex sentences, passive voice, and other issues that may make the content difficult to read or understand. Website: http://www.hemingwayapp.com/

- Canva: Canva is a free AI tool that helps businesses and organizations create professional-quality graphics and design elements for their content. It includes a wide range of templates and tools for creating infographics, social media posts, and other types of visual content. Website: https://www.canva.com/

- GPT-3: GPT-3 is a free AI tool developed by OpenAI that can be used to generate high-quality and informative content. It uses natural language processing (NLP) to analyze a given topic or input and generate human-like text based on that analysis. Website: https://openai.com/blog/gpt-3-apps/

Here are some AI tools that businesses and organizations can use to create high-quality and informative content, although they may have a cost associated with them:

- Articoolo: Articoolo is an AI tool that helps businesses and organizations generate high-quality and informative content based on a given topic or input. It uses NLP to analyze the topic and generate relevant and informative content. Website: https://www.articoolo.com/

- Wordsmith: Wordsmith is an AI tool that helps businesses and organizations generate high-quality and informative content based on a given topic or input. It uses NLP to analyze the topic and generate relevant and informative content, and includes features such as customizable templates and the ability to analyze sentiment. Website: https://www.automatedinsights.com/wordsmith

- Articulate AI: Articulate AI is an AI tool that helps businesses and organizations generate high-quality and informative content based on a given topic or input. It uses NLP to analyze the topic and generate relevant and informative content, and includes features such as customizable templates and the ability to analyze sentiment. Website: https://articulate.ai/

Overall, there are a variety of free and paid AI tools that businesses and organizations can use to create high-quality and informative content and improve the quality and quantity of external links pointing to their website. These tools can help businesses and organizations generate relevant and informative content and improve their ranking in search results.

- Build relationships with other websites: Building relationships with other websites in the industry can be a good way to acquire backlinks. This can be done through methods such as guest blogging, participating in online communities and forums, and attending industry events. By building relationships with other websites and providing value, businesses and organizations can acquire valuable backlinks that can help improve their ranking in search results.

Sample:

Here is an example of how a business can build relationships with other websites to acquire backlinks:

Let's say that a small business sells organic skincare products and wants to improve its ranking in search results for the keyword "organic skincare." One way the business can acquire backlinks is by building relationships with other websites in the industry.

One method the business could use is guest blogging. The business could reach out to websites in the skincare or beauty industry and offer to write a guest blog post on a relevant topic. By writing a high-quality and informative blog post, the business can establish itself as an expert in the industry and potentially acquire a backlink to its website.

The business could also participate in online communities and forums related to skincare and beauty. By providing valuable insights and contributing to discussions, the business can build relationships with other websites in the industry and potentially acquire backlinks.

Attending industry events is another way the business could build relationships with other websites. By networking with other professionals in the skincare and beauty industry, the business can establish itself as an expert and potentially acquire backlinks through collaborations or partnerships.

Overall, building relationships with other websites can be a valuable way for businesses and organizations to acquire backlinks and improve their ranking in search results. By providing value and establishing themselves as experts in their industry, businesses and organizations can acquire valuable backlinks that can help improve their ranking in search results.

Tools:

- Use social media: Social media platforms such as Facebook, Twitter, Snapchat, TikTok and LinkedIn can be used to promote content and acquire backlinks. By sharing content on social media and engaging with followers, businesses and organizations can drive traffic to their website and potentially acquire backlinks.

- Monitor and track backlinks: It's important to regularly monitor and track backlinks to ensure that they are high-quality and relevant. If a website has low-quality or spammy backlinks, it can negatively impact its ranking in search results. Tools such as Google Search Console and Ahrefs can be used to monitor and track backlinks and take action to remove any low-quality or spammy backlinks.

Overall, improving the quality and quantity of external links pointing to a website can be done through techniques such as creating high-quality and informative content, building relationships with other websites, using social media, and monitoring and tracking backlinks. By implementing these techniques, businesses and organizations can improve their ranking in search results and increase the visibility of their website.

Best practices for on-page optimization, including title tags, meta descriptions, and header tags

On-page optimization refers to the practice of optimizing individual web pages in order to rank higher and earn more relevant traffic in search engines. One key aspect of on-page optimization is the use of title tags, meta descriptions, and header tags. Here are some best practices for using these elements to optimize your website's pages:

1. Title tags: These are HTML elements that specify the title of a web page. Title tags should be concise, accurately describe the content of the page, and contain the primary keyword for that page. They should be placed in the head section of the HTML code for the page and should not exceed 60 characters in length.

Sample:

Here is an example of how title tags might be used to optimize a web page for a product called "Women's Running Shoes":

Title tag: Women's Running Shoes - Best Selection & Prices

In this example, the title tag accurately describes the content of the page (women's running shoes) and includes the primary keyword (running shoes). It is also concise, as it fits within the recommended length of 60 characters. This title tag could be placed in the head section of the HTML code for the page and would be displayed in the search results as the title of the page.

Other potential title tags for this page could include:

- Running Shoes for Women - Shop Our Wide Selection
- Women's Running Shoes - Comfort & Performance Guaranteed
- Best Running Shoes for Women - Find Your Perfect Pair Here

By experimenting with different title tags and A/B testing their performance, you can identify the most effective title tag for your web page and improve its chances of ranking well in search results.

Free Tools:

here are some examples of free tools that you can use to optimize a web page for a product like "women's running shoes" with the corresponding website addresses:

- Google Keyword Planner: This is a free tool offered by Google that allows you to research and compare the volume and competitiveness of different keywords. You can use this tool to help identify the best keywords to target in your website content and title tags, such as "women's running shoes" or "running shoes for women." Website address: https://ads.google.com/home/tools/keyword-planner/

- Ubersuggest: This is a free SEO tool that provides suggestions for keywords, as well as other SEO recommendations based on the website you enter. You can use this tool to get ideas for new content topics and title tags, as well as to identify potential issues with your website's SEO. Website address: https://www.ubersuggest.com/

- SEO Meta in 1 Click: This is a free browser extension that allows you to view and edit the title tags and meta descriptions of web pages. You can use this tool to quickly assess the on-page optimization of your web pages and make any necessary changes to improve their ranking in search results. Website address: https://chrome.google.com/webstore/detail/seo-meta-in-1-click/bggdcmcfppkfcjihbjbdbflgoofkmadh

- PageSpeed Insights: This is a free tool offered by Google that analyzes the performance of a web page and provides recommendations for improving its loading speed. Faster loading times can help improve the user experience and the ranking of your web pages in search results. Website address: https://developers.google.com/speed/pagespeed/insights/

There are many other free tools available that can help with on-page optimization and other aspects of SEO. These are just a few examples to get you started. It's important to do your own research and find the tools that best meet your needs and budget.

2. Meta descriptions: These are short descriptions of a web page's content that appear in the search results. Meta descriptions should accurately summarize the content of the page, contain the primary keyword for the page, and be written in a way that is attractive to users. They should be no longer than 160 characters in length.

Sample:

Here is an example of how meta descriptions might be used to optimize a web page for a product called "Men's T-Shirts":

Meta description: Shop the latest collection of men's t-shirts at our online store. Find a wide variety of styles, including graphic, solid, and striped t-shirts in sizes S-XXL.

In this example, the meta description accurately summarizes the content of the page (men's t-shirts for sale) and includes the primary keyword (t-shirts). It is also written in a way that is attractive to users, as it highlights the variety of styles and sizes available. This meta description fits within the recommended length of 160 characters and could be used to encourage users to click on the search result and visit the web page.

Other potential meta descriptions for this page could include:

- Upgrade your casual wardrobe with our men's t-shirts. Wide selection of colors and styles to choose from.
- Find the perfect t-shirt for any occasion at our online store. Shop now for men's t-shirts in sizes S-XXL.
- Get the latest men's t-shirts at unbeatable prices. Find graphic, solid, and striped styles to fit your style.

By experimenting with different meta descriptions and A/B testing their performance, you can identify the most effective meta description for your web page and improve its chances of ranking well in search results.

Free Tools:

here are some examples of free tools that you can use to test the performance of your meta descriptions and other aspects of your website's SEO, along with their website addresses:

- Google Search Console: This is a free tool offered by Google that allows you to monitor the performance of your website in search results. You can use it to see how your website is appearing in search results, identify any crawl errors or security issues, and submit your sitemap to Google. Website address: https://search.google.com/search-console

- Bing Webmaster Tools: This is a free tool offered by Bing that provides similar functionality to Google Search Console. You can use it to monitor the performance of your website in Bing search results, identify any issues with your website's crawling or indexing, and submit your sitemap to Bing. Website address: https://www.bing.com/toolbox/webmaster

- Google Analytics: This is a free tool offered by Google that allows you to track the traffic to your website and analyze user behavior. You can use it to see how users are interacting with your website, identify any issues with user experience, and track the performance of your marketing campaigns. Website address: https://www.google.com/analytics/

- Crazy Egg: This is a paid tool that provides heat maps and other visualizations to help you understand how users are interacting with your website. You can use it to identify areas of your website that are performing well or poorly and make improvements accordingly. Website address: https://www.crazyegg.com/

3. Header tags: These are HTML tags that are used to structure the content on a web page and indicate the hierarchy of the information. There are six levels of header tags, ranging from H1 (most important) to H6 (least important). It's important to use header tags correctly and consistently throughout the content on your website, as they can help search engines understand the structure and relevance of your content.

Sample:

Here is an example of how header tags might be used to structure the content on a web page for a product called "iPhone 12":

H1: iPhone 12 - The Ultimate Smartphone Experience H2: iPhone 12 Features

- 5G connectivity
- Ceramic Shield front cover
- A14 Bionic chip
- ProRAW photo format H3: iPhone 12 Design
- Super Retina XDR display
- Ceramic Shield front cover
- Aerospace-grade aluminum edges
- Water and dust resistant H4: iPhone 12 Camera
- Dual-camera system with 12MP ultra-wide and wide lenses
- Night mode, Deep Fusion, and Smart HDR 3
- ProRAW and ProRes video formats
- Dolby Vision HDR recording

In this example, the H1 tag is used to specify the main title of the web page, while the H2 and H3 tags are used to divide the content into sections and sub-sections. The H4 tags are used to further divide the content into specific topics within the sub-sections. By using header tags consistently and correctly throughout the content on the page, you can help search engines understand the structure and relevance of the content and improve the ranking of the page in search results.

Other potential header tags for this page could include H5 and H6 tags to further divide the content into even more specific topics. It's important to use header tags appropriately and not overuse them, as this can negatively impact the ranking of the page in search results.

Free Tools:

here are some examples of free tools that you can use to optimize the header tags and other aspects of your website's SEO, along with their website addresses:

- Google Search Console: This is a free tool offered by Google that allows you to monitor the performance of your website in search results. You can use it to see how your website is appearing in search results, identify any crawl errors or security issues, and submit your sitemap to Google. Website address: https://search.google.com/search-console

- Bing Webmaster Tools: This is a free tool offered by Bing that provides similar functionality to Google Search Console. You can use it to monitor the performance of your website in Bing search results, identify any issues with your website's crawling or indexing, and submit your sitemap to Bing. Website address: https://www.bing.com/toolbox/webmaster

- Google Analytics: This is a free tool offered by Google that allows you to track the traffic to your website and analyze user behavior. You can use it to see how users are interacting with your website, identify any issues with user experience, and track the performance of your marketing campaigns. Website address: https://www.google.com/analytics/

- SEMrush: This is a paid tool that provides a wide range of SEO and marketing features, including keyword research, site audit, and competitor analysis. You can use it to optimize your website's content and structure, identify potential issues with your SEO, and track the performance of your campaigns. Website address: https://www.semrush.com/

There are many other tools available that can help with SEO optimization and analysis. These are just a few examples to get you started. It's important to do your own research and find the tools that best meet your needs and

By following these best practices for title tags, meta descriptions, and header tags, you can help improve the on-page optimization of your website and increase its chances of ranking well in search results.

4. Link Building and Off-Page Optimization:

The importance of backlinks for SEO and SEM

Backlinks, also known as external links or inbound links, are links from other websites that point to your website. They are an important factor in search engine optimization (SEO) because they signal to search engines that your website is trustworthy and relevant.

Here are a few reasons why backlinks are important for SEO and search engine marketing (SEM):

1. Authority: Having backlinks from high-quality and authoritative websites can increase the credibility and perceived value of your website in the eyes of search engines. This can help improve your website's ranking in search results for relevant keywords.

Sample and Tools:

here is an example of how a business might use backlinks from high-quality and authoritative websites to improve its authority and ranking in search results for the keyword "organic skincare":

- Research potential backlink opportunities: The business uses free tools such as Google Search Console (https://search.google.com/search-console) and Bing Webmaster Tools (https://www.bing.com/toolbox/webmaster) to identify websites in the skincare or beauty industry that have high domain authority and are relevant to its industry or topic.

- Reach out to potential partners: The business reaches out to these websites and offers to write a guest blog post or contribute content in exchange for a backlink to its website. By building backlinks from these types of websites, the business can improve its credibility and perceived value in the eyes of search engines, which can help improve its ranking in search results.

- Monitor and track results: The business uses free tools such as Google Analytics (https://analytics.google.com/) to track the performance of its backlink strategy and see the impact on its website's ranking in search results.

Advanced tools such as Ahrefs (https://ahrefs.com/) and Moz (https://moz.com/) can also be useful for backlink research and analysis. These paid tools provide more advanced features and can help businesses and organizations identify and track high-quality backlink opportunities and monitor the performance of their backlink strategy.

Overall, it's important for businesses and organizations to focus on building high-quality and relevant backlinks as part of their SEO and SEM strategy. By building backlinks from authoritative and relevant websites, businesses and organizations can improve their credibility, relevance, and ranking in search results for relevant keywords.

2. Relevance: Backlinks from websites that are related to your industry or topic can help establish the relevance of your website for those topics. This can help your website rank higher in search results for relevant keywords and improve the quality of traffic to your website.

Sample and Free Tools:

here is an example of how a business might use backlinks to improve the relevance of its website for the keyword "organic skincare":

- Focus on building backlinks from websites that are related to the industry or topic of the business. For example, the business might reach out to natural health blogs or websites that focus on organic products and offer to write a guest blog post or contribute content in exchange for a backlink.

- Use tools to research potential backlink opportunities and track the performance of the backlinks. Some examples of free tools that can help with this include:

- Google Search Console: This is a free tool offered by Google that allows you to monitor the performance of your website in search results. You can use it to see the backlinks pointing to your website, identify any issues with your website's crawling or indexing, and submit your sitemap to Google. Website address: https://search.google.com/search-console

- Bing Webmaster Tools: This is a free tool offered by Bing that provides similar functionality to Google Search Console. You can use it to monitor the performance of your website in Bing search results, identify any issues with your website's crawling or indexing, and submit your sitemap to Bing. Website address: https://www.bing.com/toolbox/webmaster

Some advanced tools that can help with backlink research and analysis include:

- Ahrefs: This is a paid tool that provides a wide range of SEO and marketing features, including backlink analysis, keyword research, and site audit. You can use it to track the backlinks pointing to your website, identify potential issues with your backlink profile, and research potential backlink opportunities. Website address: https://ahrefs.com/

- Moz: This is a paid tool that provides a range of SEO and marketing features, including backlink analysis, keyword research, and site audit. You can use it to track the backlinks pointing to your website, identify potential issues with your backlink profile, and research potential backlink opportunities. Website address: https://moz.com/

Overall, it's important to focus on building high-quality and relevant backlinks as part of your SEO and SEM strategy. By building backlinks from websites that are related to your industry or topic, you can improve the relevance of your website for those topics and potentially rank higher in search results for relevant keywords. Using tools to research and track your backlinks can help you identify potential opportunities and optimize your strategy over time.

3. Traffic: Backlinks can also drive traffic to your website from other sources. If someone clicks on a backlink to your website from another website, they will be directed to your website and potentially become a visitor or customer.

Sample and Free Tools:

here are some examples of free tools that you can use to track the traffic driven to your website by backlinks, along with their website addresses:

- Google Analytics: This is a free tool offered by Google that allows you to track the traffic to your website and analyze user behavior. You can use it to see how much traffic is being driven to your website by backlinks, identify the sources of that traffic, and track the performance of your marketing campaigns. Website address: https://www.google.com/analytics/

- Bitly: This is a free tool that allows you to create and track short links to your website. You can use it to create short links for your backlinks, track the clicks on those links, and see how much traffic is being driven to your website as a result. Website address: https://bitly.com/

- LinkTracker: This is a free tool that allows you to track the clicks on your links, including backlinks. You can use it to see how much traffic is being driven to your website by backlinks, identify the sources of that traffic, and track the performance of your marketing campaigns. Website address: https://www.linktracker.com/

Here are some examples of advanced tools that you can use to track the traffic driven to your website by backlinks, along with their website addresses:

- Ahrefs: This is a paid tool that provides a wide range of SEO and marketing features, including backlink analysis, keyword research, and site audit. You can use it to track the traffic driven to your website by backlinks, identify the sources of that traffic, and research potential backlink opportunities. Website address: https://ahrefs.com/

- Moz: This is a paid tool that provides a range of SEO and marketing features, including backlink analysis, keyword research, and site audit. You can use it to track the traffic driven to your website by backlinks, identify the sources of that traffic, and research potential backlink opportunities. Website address: https://moz.com/

There are many other tools available that can help with tracking the traffic driven to your website by backlinks. These are just a few examples to get you started. It's important to do your own research and find the tools that best meet your needs and budget.

Overall, backlinks are an important factor in the ranking algorithm of search engines and can have a significant impact on the visibility and success of your website in search results. It's important to focus on building high-quality and relevant backlinks to your website as part of your SEO and SEM strategy.

Strategies for building high-quality backlinks

Building high-quality backlinks is an important part of a successful search engine optimization (SEO) and search engine marketing (SEM) strategy. High-quality backlinks can help improve the credibility, relevance, and ranking of your website in search results for relevant keywords. Here are a few strategies you can use to build high-quality backlinks:

1. Guest blogging: Reach out to relevant websites in your industry or topic and offer to write a guest blog post in exchange for a backlink to your website. This can be a

great way to build relationships with other websites and establish your expertise in your field.

Sample and Tools:

here are some examples of free and paid tools that you can use to help with guest blogging and backlink building, along with their website addresses:

Free tools:

- Google Alerts: This is a free tool offered by Google that allows you to receive notifications when new content is published online that matches certain keywords or phrases. You can use it to stay up-to-date with the latest content in your industry and identify potential opportunities for guest blogging or backlink building. Website address: https://www.google.com/alerts

- BuzzSumo: This is a paid tool that provides a range of features for content marketing and social media analysis, including the ability to see the most shared content for a specific topic or website. You can use it to identify popular websites in your industry and potentially reach out to them for guest blogging opportunities. Website address: https://buzzsumo.com/

Paid tools:

- SEMrush: This is a paid tool that provides a wide range of SEO and marketing features, including keyword research, site audit, and competitor analysis. You can use it to identify potential backlink opportunities, research the link profile of your competitors, and track the performance of your backlink campaigns. Website address: https://www.semrush.com/

- Ahrefs: This is a paid tool that provides a wide range of SEO and marketing features, including backlink analysis, keyword research, and site audit. You can use it to track the backlinks pointing to your website, identify potential issues with your backlink profile, and research potential backlink opportunities. Website address: https://ahrefs.com/

There are many other tools available that can help with guest blogging and backlink building. These are just a few examples to get you started. It's important to do your own research and find the tools that best meet your needs and budget.

2. Online communities and forums: Participate in online communities and forums related to your industry or topic and contribute valuable insights and information. This can help build relationships with other websites and may lead to opportunities for collaborations or partnerships that result in backlinks.

Sample and Tools:

here is an example of how a business might use online communities and forums to acquire backlinks, along with some suggestions for free and advanced tools that can help:

- Join relevant online communities and forums: The business joins online communities and forums related to its industry or topic, such as Reddit, Quora, or LinkedIn

Groups. It actively participates in discussions, provides valuable insights and information, and establishes itself as an expert in the field.

- Build relationships: By consistently contributing valuable content and engaging with other members of the community, the business builds relationships with other websites and professionals in the industry. This can lead to opportunities for collaborations or partnerships that result in backlinks to the business's website.

Free tools for participating in online communities and forums:

- Reddit: This is a social news and discussion website that allows users to submit and vote on content. You can use it to join relevant communities and participate in discussions related to your industry or topic. Website address: https://www.reddit.com/

- Quora: This is a question-and-answer website where users can ask and answer questions on a wide range of topics. You can use it to find and answer questions related to your industry or topic and build your reputation as an expert. Website address: https://www.quora.com/

- LinkedIn Groups: This is a feature of LinkedIn that allows users to join and participate in discussions with other professionals in their industry or topic. You can use it to join relevant groups and participate in discussions to build relationships and potentially acquire backlinks. Website address: https://www.linkedin.com/groups/

Advanced tools for participating in online communities and forums:

- Brand24: This is a paid tool that allows you to track and analyze mentions of your brand or keywords across the web, including in online communities and forums. You can use it to identify opportunities to participate in relevant discussions and build relationships with other websites and professionals in your industry. Website address: https://brand24.com/

- Mention: This is a paid tool that allows you to track and analyze mentions of your brand or keywords across the web, including in online communities and forums. You can use it to identify opportunities to participate in relevant discussions and build relationships with other websites and professionals in your industry. Website address: https://www.mention.com/

There are many other tools available that can help with participation in online communities and forums. These are just a few examples to get you started. It's important to do your own research and find the tools that best meet your needs and budget.

3. Industry events: Attend industry events and network with other professionals in your field. This can help establish your expertise and may lead to opportunities for collaborations or partnerships that result in backlinks.

Sample and Tools:

here is an example of how a business might use industry events to acquire backlinks, along with some suggestions for free and advanced tools that can help:

- Attend industry events: The business attends industry events and conferences related to its field, such as trade shows, workshops, or seminars. This allows the business to network with other professionals and establish itself as an expert in its field.

- Network with other professionals: The business takes advantage of networking opportunities at industry events to build relationships with other professionals in its field. This could include attending panel discussions, participating in roundtables, or simply chatting with other attendees at the event.

- Collaborate or partner with other websites: By building relationships with other professionals and organizations at industry events, the business may be able to secure collaborations or partnerships that result in backlinks to its website. For example, the business might collaborate on a blog post or research study with another organization and include a backlink to its website as part of the collaboration.

Here are some free and advanced tools that can help with this process:

Free tools:

- LinkedIn: This is a professional networking platform that can be used to connect with other professionals in your field and find industry events. Website address: https://www.linkedin.com/

- Eventbrite: This is a platform that allows you to search for and find industry events in your area. Website address: https://www.eventbrite.com/

Advanced tools:

- HubSpot: This is a paid marketing, sales, and customer service platform that includes a range of features for networking and event management. Website address: https://www.hubspot.com/

- Cvent: This is a paid event management platform that includes features for event registration, ticketing, and networking. Website address: https://www.cvent.com/

These are just a few examples of the many tools that are available to help you find and attend industry events and build relationships with other professionals in your field. It's important to do your own research and find the tools that best meet your needs and budget.

4. Content marketing: Create high-quality, informative, and useful content on your website and promote it through social media, email marketing, and other channels. This can help attract backlinks naturally as other websites and individuals share and link to your content.

Sample and Tools

here are some examples of free tools that you can use to help with content marketing and attract backlinks, along with their website addresses:

Free tools:

- Hootsuite: This is a social media management tool that allows you to schedule and publish content to multiple social media platforms. You can use it to promote your content and drive traffic to your website. Website address: https://hootsuite.com/

- Mailchimp: This is an email marketing platform that allows you to create and send newsletters, promotional emails, and other types of email campaigns. You can use it to promote your content and drive traffic to your website. Website address: https://mailchimp.com/

- Canva: This is a design tool that allows you to create graphics, social media posts, and other types of visual content. You can use it to create eye-catching and shareable content to promote your website and attract backlinks. Website address: https://www.canva.com/

Advanced tools:

- Ahrefs: This is a paid tool that provides a wide range of SEO and marketing features, including backlink analysis, keyword research, and site audit. You can use it to track the backlinks pointing to your website, identify potential issues with your backlink profile, and research potential backlink opportunities. Website address: https://ahrefs.com/

- Moz: This is a paid tool that provides a range of SEO and marketing features, including backlink analysis, keyword research, and site audit. You can use it to track the backlinks pointing to your website, identify potential issues with your backlink profile, and research potential backlink opportunities. Website address: https://moz.com/

- SEMrush: This is a paid tool that provides a wide range of SEO and marketing features, including keyword research, site audit, and competitor analysis. You can use it to optimize your website's content and structure, identify potential issues with your SEO, and track the performance of your campaigns. Website address: https://www.semrush.com/

There are many other tools available that can help with content marketing and backlink acquisition. These are just a few examples to get you started. It's important to do your own research and find the tools that best meet your needs and budget.

5. Broken link building: Identify broken links on other websites and offer to replace them with a link to your website. This can be a great way to build relationships with other websites and improve the user experience for their visitors.

Sample and Tools:

ere are some examples of **free tools** that you can use to identify and fix broken links on your website or on other websites, along with their website addresses:

- Google Search Console: This is a free tool offered by Google that allows you to monitor the performance of your website in search results. You can use it to identify crawl errors on your website, including broken links, and fix them to improve the user experience and search engine visibility of your website. Website address: https://search.google.com/search-console

- W3C Link Checker: This is a free tool offered by the World Wide Web Consortium (W3C) that allows you to check the links on your website for validity. You can use it to identify broken links on your website and fix them to improve the user experience and search engine visibility of your website. Website address: https://validator.w3.org/checklink

- Xenu's Link Sleuth: This is a free tool that allows you to check the links on your website for validity. You can use it to identify broken links on your website and fix them to improve the user experience and search engine visibility of your website. Website address: http://home.snafu.de/tilman/xenulink.html

- Broken Link Checker: This is a free online tool that allows you to check the links on your website for validity. You can use it to identify broken links on your website and fix them to improve the user experience and search engine visibility of your website. Website address: https://www.brokenlinkcheck.com/

Here are some examples of **advanced tools** that you can use to identify and fix broken links on other websites, along with their website addresses:

- Ahrefs: This is a paid tool that provides a wide range of SEO and marketing features, including backlink analysis, keyword research, and site audit. You can use it to identify broken links on other websites and offer to replace them with a link to your website as part of a broken link building strategy. Website address: https://ahrefs.com/

- LinkResearchTools: This is a paid tool that provides a range of SEO and marketing features, including backlink analysis, keyword research, and site audit. You can use it to identify broken links on other websites and offer to replace them with a link to your website as part of a broken link building strategy. Website address: https://www.linkresearchtools.com/

- SEMrush: This is a paid tool that provides a wide range of SEO and marketing features, including backlink analysis, keyword research, and site audit. You can use it to identify broken links on other websites and offer to

Overall, it's important to focus on building high-quality and relevant backlinks as part of your SEO and SEM strategy. By providing value and establishing yourself as an expert in your field, you can attract high-quality backlinks that can help improve your credibility, relevance, and ranking in search results.

Techniques for improving the quality and quantity of external links pointing to your website

Here are some techniques that businesses and organizations can use to improve the quality and quantity of external links pointing to their website:

1. Create high-quality content: One of the most effective ways to attract backlinks to your website is to create high-quality and valuable content that people will naturally want to link to. This might include blog posts, articles, infographics, videos, or other types of content that are informative, engaging, and useful to your target audience.

Sample and Tools:

here are some examples of free tools that you can use to create high-quality content and attract backlinks to your website, along with their website addresses:

- Google Docs: This is a free tool offered by Google that allows you to create and collaborate on documents, spreadsheets, and presentations. You can use it to write blog posts, articles, and other types of content and share them with others for feedback and collaboration. Website address: https://www.google.com/docs/about/

- Canva: This is a free tool that allows you to create professional-quality graphics and designs. You can use it to create infographics, social media images, and other types of visual content to share on your website or social media channels. Website address: https://www.canva.com/

- Hootsuite: This is a free tool that allows you to manage your social media accounts and schedule posts in advance. You can use it to share your content on social media and reach a wider audience. Website address: https://hootsuite.com/

Here are some examples of advanced tools that you can use to create high-quality content and attract backlinks to your website, along with their website addresses:

- CoSchedule Headline Analyzer: This is a paid tool that analyzes the quality and effectiveness of your headlines and offers suggestions for improvement. You can use it to optimize your headlines for SEO and social media performance and increase the chances of your content being shared and linked to. Website address: https://coschedule.com/headline-analyzer

- BuzzSumo: This is a paid tool that allows you to research and analyze the most shared and popular content on the web. You can use it to identify content trends and opportunities, as well as to track the performance of your own content. Website address: https://buzzsumo.com/

- SEMrush: This is a paid tool that provides a wide range of SEO and marketing features, including keyword research, site audit, and competitor analysis. You can use it to optimize your website's content and structure, identify potential issues with your SEO, and track the performance of your campaigns. Website address: https://www.semrush.com/

There are many other tools available that can help with content creation and backlink acquisition. These are just a few examples to get you started. It's important to do your own research and find the tools that best meet your needs and budget.

2. Promote your content: Once you have created high-quality content, it's important to promote it to get the word out. You can do this through social media, email marketing, outreach to relevant websites or influencers, and other tactics. The more people who see your content, the more likely it is that you will acquire backlinks.

Sample and Tools:

Here are some examples of free and advanced tools that you can use to promote your content and acquire backlinks, along with their website addresses:

Free tools:

- Social media platforms: You can use social media platforms like Facebook, Twitter, LinkedIn, and

Instagram to promote your content and drive traffic to your website. These platforms are free to use and allow you to reach a wide audience.

- Email marketing: You can use email marketing tools like Mailchimp or Constant Contact to create and send newsletters or promotional emails to your subscribers. These tools allow you to target specific segments of your audience and track the performance of your campaigns.

- Outreach: You can use tools like BuzzSumo or Mention to identify websites or influencers in your industry and reach out to them to promote your content. These tools allow you to find relevant websites and contact information and track the performance of your outreach efforts.

Advanced tools:

- SEMrush: This is a paid tool that provides a wide range of SEO and marketing features, including keyword research, site audit, and competitor analysis. You can use it to optimize your content and identify potential backlink opportunities. Website address: https://www.semrush.com/

- Ahrefs: This is a paid tool that provides a wide range of SEO and marketing features, including backlink analysis, keyword research, and site audit. You can use it to track the backlinks pointing to your website, identify potential issues with your backlink profile, and research potential backlink opportunities. Website address: https://ahrefs.com/

- Moz: This is a paid tool that provides a range of SEO and marketing features, including backlink analysis, keyword research, and site audit. You can use it to track the backlinks pointing to your website, identify potential issues with your backlink profile, and research potential backlink opportunities. Website address: https://moz.com/

There are many other tools available that can help with content promotion and backlink acquisition. These are just a few examples to get you started. It's important to do your own research and find the tools that best meet your needs and budget.

3. Participate in online communities and forums: Participating in online communities and forums related to your industry or topic can help you build relationships with other websites and potentially acquire backlinks. You can contribute valuable insights and information to discussions, answer questions, and provide valuable resources to help establish yourself as an expert in your field.

Sample and Tools:

Here is an example of how a business might participate in online communities and forums to acquire backlinks and improve its ranking in search results:

- Research relevant communities and forums: The business conducts research to identify online communities and forums related to its industry or topic.

This could include industry-specific forums, social media groups, or discussion boards on websites related to the business's niche.

- Contribute valuable insights and resources: The business actively participates in these communities and forums by contributing valuable insights and information to discussions, answering questions, and providing valuable resources. By consistently providing value and establishing itself as an expert in the industry, the business can build relationships with other websites and potentially acquire backlinks through collaborations or partnerships.

Free tools that can help with this process include:

- Reddit: This is a social news and discussion website that allows users to participate in a variety of forums and communities. You can use it to find communities related to your industry or topic and contribute valuable insights and resources. Website address: https://www.reddit.com/

- Quora: This is a question-and-answer website that allows users to ask and answer questions on a variety of topics. You can use it to find questions related to your industry or topic and provide valuable answers and resources. Website address: https://www.quora.com/

- LinkedIn Groups: LinkedIn is a professional networking website that allows users to join and participate in groups related to their industry or interests. You can use it to find groups related to your industry or topic and contribute valuable insights and resources. Website address: https://www.linkedin.com/groups/

Advanced tools that can help with this process include:

- Ahrefs: This is a paid tool that provides a wide range of SEO and marketing features, including backlink analysis, keyword research, and site audit. You can use it to track the backlinks pointing to your website, identify potential issues with your backlink profile, and research potential backlink opportunities. Website address: https://ahrefs.com/

- Moz: This is a paid tool that provides a range of SEO and marketing features, including backlink analysis, keyword research, and site audit. You can use it to track the backlinks pointing to your website, identify potential issues with your backlink profile, and research potential backlink opportunities. Website address: https://moz.com/

Again, these are just a few examples of tools that you can use to participate in online communities and forums and build backlinks. It's important to do your own research and find the tools that best meet your needs and budget.

4. Attend industry events: Attending industry events and networking with other professionals in your field can help you build relationships with other websites and potentially acquire backlinks. You can establish yourself as an expert and explore opportunities for collaborations or partnerships that might lead to backlinks.

Sample and Tools:

here are some examples of free and advanced tools that you can use to help build relationships and acquire backlinks through industry events, along with their website addresses:

Free tools:

- LinkedIn: This is a professional networking platform that allows you to connect with other professionals in your industry and explore opportunities for collaboration. You can use it to find and attend industry events, network with other professionals, and build relationships that might lead to backlinks. Website address: https://www.linkedin.com/

- Eventbrite: This is a platform that allows you to search for and register for events in your area. You can use it to find industry events in your area and plan to attend them to network with other professionals and potentially acquire backlinks. Website address: https://www.eventbrite.com/

Advanced tools:

- HubSpot: This is a paid customer relationship management (CRM) platform that provides a range of marketing and sales features, including event management. You can use it to plan and promote events, register attendees, and track the performance of your events. Website address: https://www.hubspot.com/

- Cvent: This is a paid event management platform that provides a range of features for planning and managing events, including registration, ticketing, and lead generation. You can use it to plan and promote events, track the performance of your events, and follow up with attendees to explore opportunities for collaboration or partnerships that might lead to backlinks. Website address: https://www.cvent.com/

There are many other tools available that can help with event management and networking. These are just a few examples to get you started. It's important to do your own research and find the tools that best meet your needs and budget.

5. Use social media: Social media platforms can be a great way to promote your content and build relationships with other websites. By sharing your content on social media and engaging with others in your industry, you can increase the visibility of your website and potentially acquire backlinks.

Sample and Tools:

here are some examples of free tools and advanced tools that you can use to promote your content and build relationships on social media, along with their website addresses:

Free tools:

- Hootsuite: This is a social media management tool that allows you to schedule and publish content to multiple social media platforms, including Facebook, Twitter, LinkedIn, and Instagram. You can also use it to monitor social media conversations and engage with other users. Website address: https://hootsuite.com/

- Buffer: This is a social media management tool that allows you to schedule and publish content to multiple social media platforms, including Facebook, Twitter, LinkedIn, and Instagram. You can also use it to analyze the performance of your social media campaigns and identify trends. Website address: https://buffer.com/

- Canva: This is a graphic design tool that allows you to create social media graphics, infographics, and other visual content. You can use it to create engaging and shareable content for your social media profiles and pages. Website address: https://www.canva.com/

Advanced tools:

- Sprout Social: This is a paid social media management and analytics tool that offers a range of features for managing and analyzing your social media presence. You can use it to schedule and publish content, engage with users, and track the performance of your campaigns. Website address: https://www.sproutsocial.com/

- SocialBee: This is a paid social media management tool that offers a range of features for managing and analyzing your social media presence. You can use it to schedule and publish content, engage with users, and track the performance of your campaigns. Website address: https://www.socialbee.io/

- Agorapulse: This is a paid social media management tool that offers a range of features for managing and analyzing your social media presence. You can use it to schedule and publish content, engage with users, and track the performance of your campaigns. Website address: https://www.agorapulse.com/

These are just a few examples of the many tools available for promoting your content and building relationships on social media. It's important to do your own research and find the tools that best meet your needs and budget.

5. Local SEO and Maps Optimization:

The role of local SEO in attracting customers from a specific geographic area

Local SEO refers to the practice of optimizing your online presence to attract customers from a specific geographic area, such as a city, region, or country. It's a key aspect of search engine optimization (SEO) that helps businesses and organizations attract customers who are searching for products or services in their local area.

There are several strategies and techniques that businesses and organizations can use to improve their local SEO and attract customers from a specific geographic area. These include:

1. Optimizing your website for local keywords: By including local keywords in your website content and meta tags, you can help search engines understand the relevance of your website for local search queries.

Sample and Tools:

here are some examples of free tools and advanced tools that you can use to optimize your website for local keywords, along with their website addresses:

Free tools:

- Google Keyword Planner: This is a free tool offered by Google that allows you to research and find relevant keywords for your website. You can use it to find local keywords that are related to your business or industry and include them in your website content and meta tags. Website address: https://ads.google.com/home/tools/keyword-planner/

- Ubersuggest: This is a free keyword research tool that allows you to find relevant keywords for your website. You can use it to find local keywords that are related to your business or industry and include them in your website content and meta tags. Website address: https://www.ubersuggest.com/

- Keywords Everywhere: This is a free keyword research tool that allows you to find relevant keywords for your website. You can use it to find local keywords that are related to your business or industry and include them in your website content and meta tags. Website address: https://keywords everywhere.com/

Advanced tools:

- Ahrefs: This is a paid keyword research and SEO tool that offers a range of features for finding and optimizing keywords. You can use it to find local keywords that are related to your business or industry and include them in your website content and meta tags. Website address: https://ahrefs.com/

- SEMrush: This is a paid keyword research and SEO tool that offers a range of features for finding and optimizing keywords. You can use it to find local keywords that are related to your business or industry and include them in your website content and meta tags. Website address: https://www.semrush.com/

- KWFinder: This is a paid keyword research and SEO tool that offers a range of features for finding and optimizing keywords. You can use it to find local keywords that are related to your business or industry and include them in your website content and meta tags. Website address: https://www.kwfinder.com/

These are just a few examples of the many tools available for optimizing your website for local keywords. It's important to do your own research and find the tools that best meet your needs and budget.

2. Building citations: Citations are mentions of your business name, address, and phone number (NAP) on other websites. By building citations on local directories and review sites, you can improve your visibility in local search results.

Sampe and Tools:

here are some examples of free and advanced tools that you can use to build citations and improve your visibility in local search results, along with their website addresses:

Free tools:

- Google My Business: This is a free tool offered by Google that allows you to manage your business's presence on Google Maps and in Google search results. You can use it to create and verify your business listing, add photos, and respond to reviews. Website address: https://www.google.com/business/

- Yelp: This is a popular review site that allows businesses to create and manage their listings. You can use it to add your business's name, address, phone number, and other information, as well as respond to reviews and interact with customers. Website address: https://www.yelp.com/

- Yellow Pages: This is a local business directory that allows businesses to create and manage their listings. You can use it to add your business's name, address, phone number, and other information, as well as respond to reviews and interact with customers. Website address: https://www.yellowpages.com/

Advanced tools:

- Yext: This is a paid tool that provides a range of local search and citation management features. You can use it to manage your business's listings on various local directories and review sites, as well as track your online presence and performance. Website address: https://www.yext.com/

- BrightLocal: This is a paid tool that provides a range of local search and citation management features. You can use it to manage your business's listings on various local directories and review sites, as well as track your online presence and performance. Website address: https://www.brightlocal.com/

- Moz Local: This is a paid tool that provides a range of local search and citation management features. You can use it to manage your business's listings on various local directories and review sites, as well as track your online presence and performance. Website address: https://moz.com/local

There are many other tools available that can help with local search and citation management. These are just a few examples to get you started. It's important to do your own research and find the tools that best meet your needs and budget.

3. Optimizing your Google My Business listing: Google My Business is a free tool that allows businesses to manage their online presence on Google, including search and maps. By optimizing your Google My Business listing, you can improve your visibility in local search results and attract customers from your specific geographic area.

Sample and Tools:

here are some examples of free and advanced tools that you can use to optimize your Google My Business listing and improve your visibility in local search results, along with their website addresses:

Free tools:

- Google My Business: This is a free tool offered by Google that allows businesses to manage their online presence on Google, including search and maps. You can use it to create or claim your business listing, add photos and information about your business, and respond to reviews. Website address: https://www.google.com/business/

- Yext: This is a paid tool that provides a range of local SEO and marketing features, including listing management, review management, and citation building. You can use it to optimize your business listing on Google and other local directories, manage your online reviews, and build citations to improve your visibility in local search results. Website address: https://www.yext.com/

Advanced tools:

- BrightLocal: This is a paid tool that provides a range of local SEO and marketing features, including citation building, review management, and local keyword research. You can use it to optimize your business listing on Google and other local directories, manage your online reviews, and research the best keywords to target in your local market. Website address: https://www.brightlocal.com/

- Moz Local: This is a paid tool that provides a range of local SEO and marketing features, including listing management, citation building, and review management. You can use it to optimize your business listing on Google and other local directories, build citations to improve your visibility in local search results, and manage your online reviews. Website address: https://moz.com/products/local

There are many other tools available that can help with local SEO and listing management. These are just a few examples to get you started. It's important to do your own research and find the tools that best meet your needs and budget.

4. Building local backlinks: Backlinks from websites that are based in your local area can help improve your local SEO. You can build local backlinks by contributing content to local blogs or websites, participating in local events or organizations, and building relationships with other local businesses.

Sample and Tools:

here is an example of how a local business might use backlinks to improve its local SEO:

- Local blogs and websites: The business reaches out to local blogs or websites and offers to write a guest blog post or contribute content in exchange for a backlink. By building backlinks from these types of websites, the business can improve its credibility and relevance in the eyes of local search engines, which can help improve its ranking in local search results.

- Local events and organizations: The business participates in local events or organizations and builds relationships with other local businesses. By building these relationships, the business may be able to acquire backlinks through collaborations or partnerships.

Here are some examples of free tools that you can use to help manage and track your local backlink strategy, along with their website addresses:

- Google My Business: This is a free tool offered by Google that allows you to manage your business listing on Google Maps and Google search results. You can use it to update your business information, respond to reviews, and track your performance in local search results. Website address: https://www.google.com/business/

- Bing Places for Business: This is a free tool offered by Bing that allows you to manage your business listing on Bing Maps and Bing search results. You can use it to update your business information, respond to reviews, and track your performance in local search results. Website address: https://www.bingplaces.com/

Here are some examples of advanced tools that you can use to help manage and track your local backlink strategy, along with their website addresses:

- BrightLocal: This is a paid tool that provides a range of local SEO and marketing features, including local citation tracking, local keyword research, and local review management. You can use it to track the performance of your local business in search results, identify potential issues with your local SEO, and research potential local backlink opportunities. Website address: https://www.brightlocal.com/

- Moz Local: This is a paid tool that provides a range of local SEO and marketing features, including local citation tracking, local keyword research, and local review management. You can use it to track the performance of your local business in search results, identify potential issues with your local SEO, and research potential local backlink opportunities. Website address: https://moz.com/local

There are many other tools available that can help with local backlink management and analysis. These are just a few examples to get you started. It's important to do your own research and find the tools that best meet your needs and budget.

Overall, local SEO is a key aspect of SEO that helps businesses and organizations attract customers from a specific geographic area. By optimizing your online presence for local search queries and building a strong local presence, you can improve your visibility in local search results and attract more customers from your target geographic area.

Techniques for optimizing your website and online presence for local search results

here are some techniques that businesses and organizations can use to optimize their website and online presence for local search results:

1. Claim and optimize your Google My Business listing: This is a free tool offered by Google that allows businesses to manage their presence on Google Maps and in local search results. By claiming and optimizing your business listing, you can provide accurate and up-to-date information about your business, including your location, hours of operation, contact information, and services or products offered.

Example and Tools:

Here is an example of how to claim and optimize your Google My Business (GMB) listing using **free tools**:

1. Go to https://www.google.com/business/ and click on the "Start now" button.
2. Sign in with your Google account, or create a new one if you don't have one.
3. Follow the prompts to search for your business. If your business is already listed, you can claim it by clicking on the listing and following the prompts. If it is not listed, you can add it by clicking on the "Add your business" button and entering the necessary information.
4. Once you have claimed or added your business, you can optimize your GMB listing by providing as much accurate and up-to-date information as possible, including your location, hours of operation, contact

information, and services or products offered. You can also add photos and videos to help showcase your business to potential customers.

Here are some **advanced tools** that you can use to further optimize your GMB listing:

- BrightLocal: This tool offers a range of local SEO services, including GMB optimization. You can sign up for a free trial at https://www.brightlocal.com/local-seo-tools/google-my-business/ to see how it can help improve your GMB listing.

- Yext: This tool offers a range of local SEO and online reputation management services, including GMB optimization. You can sign up for a free trial at https://www.yext.com/ to see how it can help improve your GMB listing.

- Moz Local: This tool offers a range of local SEO services, including GMB optimization. You can sign up for a free trial at https://moz.com/products/local to see how it can help improve your GMB listing.

2. Include local keywords and phrases in your website content: Local keywords and phrases, such as the name of your city or region, can help search engines understand the relevance of your website for local search results. Make sure to include these keywords and phrases in your website's content, including your title tags, meta descriptions, and header tags.

Example with free tools:

- Google Keyword Planner: This tool can help you identify relevant local keywords and phrases to include in your website content. Simply enter your location and industry, and the tool will generate a list of suggested keywords. You can use the tool for free by creating a Google Ads account. https://ads.google.com/home/tools/keyword-planner/
- SEMrush: This tool provides keyword suggestions based on your website's content and industry. It also shows the search volume and competition level for each keyword. You can use the tool for free by creating a SEMrush account. https://www.semrush.com/

Example with advanced tools:

- Ahrefs: This tool is a comprehensive SEO tool that offers keyword research features. It provides a list of relevant keywords based on your website's content and industry, along with search volume and competition level. You can use the tool by purchasing a subscription plan. https://www.ahrefs.com/

- Moz: This tool provides keyword research and analysis features, including a list of relevant keywords and their search volume and competition level. You can use the tool by purchasing a subscription plan. https://moz.com/products/pro/keyword-explorer

3. Build local backlinks: Backlinks from websites that are based in your local area can help improve your local SEO. You can build local backlinks by contributing

content to local blogs or websites, participating in local events or organizations, and building relationships with other local businesses.

4. Encourage customer reviews: Positive customer reviews can help improve your local SEO and credibility in the eyes of both customers and search engines. Encourage your customers to leave reviews on your Google My Business listing, Yelp, and other local review platforms.

Free tools:

- Google My Business: https://www.google.com/business/
- Yelp: https://www.yelp.com/

To encourage customer reviews using these free tools, you can:

1. Add a link to your Google My Business listing on your website, email signatures, and social media profiles. This will make it easy for customers to leave reviews on your Google My Business page.
2. Include a review request in your email or snail mail communications with customers. You can also post about it on your social media channels and ask customers to leave a review on your Google My Business page or Yelp.
3. Offer an incentive for customers who leave a review. This could be a discount or a special offer.

Advanced tools:

- Reputation.com: https://www.reputation.com/
- Trustpilot: https://www.trustpilot.com/

To encourage customer reviews using these advanced tools, you can:

1. Use Reputation.com's review generation feature to send automated review requests to customers after they make a purchase or visit your business.
2. Set up a Trustpilot account and add a widget to your website that allows customers to leave reviews directly on your website.
3. Monitor your reviews on these platforms and respond to all customer feedback, whether positive or negative. This shows that you value customer feedback and are willing to listen to their concerns.

5. Optimize your website for mobile devices: Many local searches are conducted on mobile devices, so it's important to make sure that your website is optimized for mobile viewing. This includes making sure that your website is responsive (meaning it adjusts to fit different screen sizes), has a fast loading speed, and is easy to navigate on a small

Free Tools:

- Google's Mobile-Friendly Test (https://search.google.com/test/mobile-friendly): This tool allows you to enter your website's URL and check if it is optimized for mobile devices. It will provide a report on any issues that need to be fixed, such as slow loading speed or unresponsive design.

- W3C's MobileOK Checker (https://validator.w3.org/mobile-ok-checker): This tool checks your website's design, layout, and content to ensure that it is optimized for mobile viewing. It will provide a list of any issues that need to be addressed, such as small font size or cluttered layout.

Advanced Tools:

- Lighthouse (https://developers.google.com/web/tools/lighthouse): This tool, developed by Google, allows you to perform a thorough audit of your website's performance, including its mobile-friendliness. It provides a detailed report on any issues that need to be fixed, such as slow loading speed or unresponsive design.

- Mobify (https://www.mobify.com/): This tool allows you to create a custom mobile version of your website, ensuring that it is optimized for viewing on all mobile devices. It offers advanced features such as the ability to customize the layout and design of your mobile site, as well as integrations with popular e-commerce platforms.

Best practices for optimizing your business listing on Google Maps

There are several best practices for optimizing your business listing on Google Maps:

1. Claim your listing: Make sure you have claimed your business listing on Google Maps so that you can update the information and respond to customer reviews.

   - **Free Tool**: Google My Business (https://www.google.com/business/)
   - **Advanced Tool**: Moz Local (https://moz.com/products/local)

2. Add accurate information: Ensure that all the information on your listing, such as your business name, address, and phone number, is accurate and up-to-date.

   - **Free Tool**: Google My Business (https://www.google.com/business/)
   - **Advanced Tool**: Moz Local (https://moz.com/products/local)

3. Use relevant categories: Choose categories that accurately reflect your business and its products or services. This will help customers find you when searching for specific products or services.

   - **Free Tool**: Google My Business (https://www.google.com/business/)
   - **Advanced Tool**: Moz Local (https://moz.com/products/local)

4. Add photos: Add high-quality photos of your business and its products or services to your listing. This will help customers get a sense of what you offer and make your listing more appealing.

- **Free Tool**: Google My Business (https://www.google.com/business/)
- **Advanced Tool**: Moz Local (https://moz.com/products/local)

5. Encourage customer reviews: Encourage customers to leave reviews on your business listing. Positive reviews can improve your ranking on Google Maps and help attract more customers.

    - **Free Tool**: Google My Business (https://www.google.com/business/)
    - **Advanced Tool**: Moz Local (https://moz.com/products/local)

6. Use keywords: Include relevant keywords in your business description to help customers find your business when searching on Google Maps.

    - **Free Tool**: Google My Business (https://www.google.com/business/)
    - **Advanced Tool**: Moz Local (https://moz.com/products/local)

7. Use special offers: If you have any special offers or promotions, make sure to include them on your business listing to attract more customers.

    - **Free Tool**: Google My Business (https://www.google.com/business/)
    - **Advanced Tool**: Moz Local (https://moz.com/products/local)

6. Technical SEO:

The importance of technical SEO for the overall performance and visibility of your website

Technical SEO plays a crucial role in the overall performance and visibility of a website. It helps to ensure that search engines can easily crawl and index a website, leading to higher search engine rankings and increased visibility.

Some of the key benefits of technical SEO include:

1. Improved site speed: A faster loading website not only leads to a better user experience, but it also helps to improve search engine rankings.

Sample and Free Tools:

One way to improve site speed through technical SEO is by using a tool like GTmetrix (https://gtmetrix.com/). This free tool analyzes a website's speed and provides recommendations for improvement, such as optimizing images and minifying code. Advanced tools like Pingdom (https://www.pingdom.com/) and WebPageTest (https://www.webpagetest.org/) also offer more in-depth analysis and performance monitoring.

2. Mobile-friendliness: With more and more people accessing the internet through their smartphones, it is important that a website is mobile-friendly. Technical SEO helps to optimize a website for mobile devices, ensuring that it is easily accessible to all users.

Sample and Free Tools:

To check the mobile-friendliness of a website, the Google Mobile-Friendly Test (https://search.google.com/test/mobile-friendly) is a free tool that provides a quick and easy analysis. Advanced tools like MobileMoxie (https://www.mobilemoxie.com/) and Lighthouse (https://developers.google.com/web/tools/lighthouse/) offer more comprehensive analysis and optimization suggestions.

3. Improved security: Technical SEO helps to secure a website and protect it from cyber attacks. This is important for both the website owner and the users, as it helps to protect sensitive information and maintain trust in the website.

Sample and Free Tools:

One way to improve website security through technical SEO is by using a tool like SSL Labs (https://www.ssllabs.com/). This free tool analyzes a website's SSL certificate and provides recommendations for improvement. Advanced tools like Sucuri (https://sucuri.net/) and Cloudflare (https://www.cloudflare.com/) offer more comprehensive security solutions, including malware scanning and protection against cyber attacks.

4. Better user experience: Technical SEO helps to improve the overall user experience on a website by ensuring that it is easy to navigate, loads quickly, and is mobile-friendly.

Sample and Tools:

To improve the user experience on a website, tools like UserTesting (https://www.usertesting.com/) and Crazy Egg (https://www.crazyegg.com/) offer user testing and heatmap analysis to identify areas of improvement. Advanced tools like FullStory (https://www.fullstory.com/) and Hotjar (https://www.hotjar.com/) offer more in-depth user behavior analysis and optimization suggestions.

Overall, technical SEO is an essential aspect of website performance and visibility. Without proper technical SEO, a website may struggle to rank well in search engine results and may not be easily accessible to users. By investing in technical SEO, a website can improve its performance, visibility, and user experience, leading to increased traffic and conversions.

Common technical issues that can impact your SEO and how to fix them

There are several common technical issues that can impact your SEO, including:

1. Slow loading times: If your website takes too long to load, it can negatively impact your SEO because search engines favor fast loading websites. To fix this issue, you can optimize your images, reduce the number of plugins, and enable caching.

Example and Tools:

Using GTmetrix to analyze website speed and identify areas for improvement.

- **Free Tools**: GTmetrix (https://gtmetrix.com/), PageSpeed Insights (https://developers.google.com/speed/pagespeed/insights/)

- **Advanced Tools**: Pingdom (https://www.pingdom.com/), WebPageTest (https://www.webpagetest.org/)

2. Broken links: Broken links can cause your website to lose credibility in the eyes of search engines. To fix this issue, you can use tools like Broken Link Checker to identify and fix broken links.

Example and Tools:

Using Broken Link Checker to scan a website for broken links and fix them.

- **Free Tools**: Broken Link Checker (https://www.brokenlinkcheck.com/), Dead Link Checker (https://www.deadlinkchecker.com/)

- **Advanced Tools**: Screaming Frog (https://www.screamingfrog.co.uk/broken-links/), Ahrefs (https://ahrefs.com/)

3. Duplicate content: Having duplicate content on your website can lead to a decrease in search engine rankings. To fix this issue, you can use the canonical tag to indicate to search engines which version of the content should be indexed.

Example and Tools:

Using Siteliner to scan a website for duplicate content and resolve any issues.

- **Free Tools**: Siteliner (https://www.siteliner.com/), Copyscape (https://www.copyscape.com/)

- **Advanced Tools**: Ahrefs (https://ahrefs.com/), SEMrush (https://www.semrush.com/)

4. Poor mobile experience: With more and more users accessing the internet through mobile devices, it is important to ensure that your website is mobile-friendly. To fix this issue, you can use Google's Mobile-Friendly Test tool to identify any problems and make necessary changes.

Example and Tools:

Using Google's Mobile-Friendly Test tool to determine if a website is mobile-friendly and make necessary improvements.

- **Free Tools**: Google Mobile-Friendly Test (https://search.google.com/test/mobile-friendly), MobileMoxie (https://www.mobilemoxie.com/tools/mobile-friendliness-test/)

- **Advanced Tools**: UserTesting (https://www.usertesting.com/), BrowserStack (https://www.browserstack.com/)

5. Lack of keyword optimization: Keywords are an important factor in SEO, and it is essential to include them in your website's content and meta tags. To fix this issue, you can conduct keyword research and incorporate relevant keywords into your website's content.

Example and Tools:

Using Google's Keyword Planner to research and select relevant keywords to include in website content and meta tags.

- **Free Tools**: Google Keyword Planner (https://ads.google.com/home/tools/keyword-planner/), Ubersuggest (https://neilpatel.com/ubersuggest/)

- **Advanced Tools:** Ahrefs (https://ahrefs.com/), SEMrush (https://www.semrush.com/)

By addressing these common technical issues, you can improve your website's SEO and increase its visibility in search engine results.

Techniques for improving the crawlability, indexability, and loading speed of your website

1. Use clear and descriptive URLs: You can use the free tool Screaming Frog SEO Spider (https://www.screamingfrog.co.uk/seo-spider/) to audit your website's URLs and identify any that are too long or contain unnecessary characters. For advanced options, you can use the paid tool Ahrefs (https://www.ahrefs.com/) to analyze the performance of your URLs and suggest ways to improve them.

2. Include a sitemap: The free tool XML-Sitemaps.com (https://www.xml-sitemaps.com/) allows you to generate a sitemap for your website and submit it to Google. For advanced options, you can use the paid tool DeepCrawl (https://www.deepcrawl.com/) to create and optimize your sitemap and improve the crawlability of your website.

3. Use header tags: The free tool SEO META in 1 Click (https://chrome.google.com/webstore/detail/seo-meta-

in-1-click/ahhdcmibdiihbjhednkfjieamkcjbggg) allows you to check the header tags on your website and ensure that they are being used correctly. For advanced options, you can use the paid tool SEMrush (https://www.semrush.com/) to analyze the header tags on your website and make recommendations for improvement.

4. Optimize images: The free tool JPEG Optimizer (https://www.jpeg-optimizer.com/) allows you to compress and resize images before uploading them to your website, improving the loading speed of your pages. For advanced options, you can use the paid tool Adobe Photoshop (https://www.adobe.com/products/photoshop.html) to optimize images and make additional edits as needed.

5. Use a CDN: The free tool Cloudflare (https://www.cloudflare.com/) offers a CDN service that you can use to improve the loading speed of your website. For advanced options, you can use the paid tool Akamai (https://www.akamai.com/) to set up a CDN and customize its settings to meet your specific needs.

6. Use caching: The free tool W3 Total Cache (https://wordpress.org/plugins/w3-total-cache/) allows you to enable caching on your website and improve its loading speed. For advanced options, you can use the paid tool Cloudflare (https://www.cloudflare.com/) to customize the caching settings on your website and optimize its performance.

7. Minimize redirects: The free tool Redirect Path (https://chrome.google.com/webstore/detail/redirect-

path/aomidfkchockcldhbkggjokdkkebmdll) allows you to identify any redirects on your website and suggest ways to minimize their number. For advanced options, you can use the paid tool Ahrefs (https://www.ahrefs.com/) to analyze the redirects on your website and make recommendations for improvement.

7. Paid Search and PPC Advertising:

Introduction to paid search and PPC advertising

Paid search and PPC (pay-per-click) advertising is a form of online advertising in which advertisers pay a fee each time their ad is clicked. This method of advertising is commonly used to drive traffic to a website or promote a product or service.

Paid search advertising is generally conducted through search engines like Google and Bing. Advertisers create and place ads that appear when someone searches for specific keywords or phrases. Advertisers bid on these keywords, and the ad with the highest bid will appear at the top of the search results.

PPC advertising can also be done on other websites or platforms, such as social media, where ads are displayed to a targeted audience. In these cases, advertisers pay for the ad to be displayed to a certain number of people or for a certain number of clicks.

An example of paid search and PPC advertising is a clothing retailer creating an ad campaign on Google Ads. The retailer would choose specific keywords, such as "women's dresses" or "summer clothing," and bid on them to have their ad appear at the top of the search results when someone searches for those keywords. When a user clicks on the ad, they will be taken to the retailer's website and the retailer will pay a fee to Google.

The retailer can also set a budget for the ad campaign, deciding how much they are willing to spend on the ads per day or per month. The ad will only be shown until the budget has been reached, and the retailer can adjust the budget or the keywords at any time to optimize the campaign's performance.

PPC advertising can also be done on other platforms, such as social media. For example, the clothing retailer could create an ad on Facebook targeting users in a specific location, age range, or with certain interests. The ad will be shown to those users and the retailer will pay a fee each time the ad is clicked or when a certain number of users have seen the ad.

To calculate the cost of a paid search and PPC advertising campaign, the retailer will need to consider their budget and the cost per click (CPC) of the keywords they are bidding on. For example, if the retailer has a budget of $1,000 per month and they choose 10 keywords with an average CPC of $0.50, they will pay $0.50 each time someone clicks on their ad when searching for one of those keywords. If the retailer's ad receives an average of 50 clicks per day, this will cost them $25 per day ($0.50 x 50 clicks = $25). Over the course of a month, this will add up to $750 in ad spend ($25 x 30 days = $750).

If the retailer also creates a PPC campaign on a social media platform, such as Facebook, and spends an additional $200 per month on this campaign, the total budget for their paid search and PPC advertising campaigns will be $950 per month ($750 + $200 = $950).

Paid search and PPC advertising can be an effective way to reach a specific audience and drive traffic to a website, but it is important to carefully manage and monitor the campaigns to ensure that they are producing the desired results. Advertisers should also be aware of the potential risks of fraudulent clicks and other types of ad fraud.

Websites where this task can be done include Google Ads, Bing Ads, and social media platforms such as Facebook and Instagram.

In conclusion, paid search and PPC advertising is a form of online advertising that allows advertisers to pay a fee each time their ad is clicked. This method can be effective in driving traffic to a website and promoting a product or service, but it is important to carefully

Setting up and managing a PPC campaign

Setting up and managing a PPC (pay-per-click) campaign involves a few key steps:

1. Define your target audience: Who do you want to reach with your campaign? Consider factors such as demographics, location, and interests.

Example and Free Tools:

To define your target audience for a PPC (pay-per-click) campaign, you can use a variety of tools and resources. Here are a few **free options**:

- Google Analytics: This tool allows you to track and analyze data on your website visitors, including demographics, location, and interests. You can use this information to better understand your existing audience and identify potential target audiences for your PPC campaign. https://www.google.com/analytics/

- Google Ads Audience Insights: This tool, available within the Google Ads platform, allows you to research specific audiences and see how they interact with your ads. You can use this information to refine your targeting and reach a more relevant audience. https://ads.google.com/home/tools/audience-insights/

- Social media analytics: Many social media platforms offer analytics tools that allow you to track and analyze data on your followers or users who engage with your content. You can use this information to learn more about your audience and identify potential target audiences for your PPC campaign.

Advanced tools with a cost include:

- Market research platforms: Companies like Forrester and Gartner offer market research and analysis services that can help you understand your target audience and identify potential target markets for your PPC campaign. Prices for these services vary.

- Audience targeting platforms: Tools like LiveRamp and BlueKai allow you to create and target specific audiences based on data points such as demographics, location, and interests. Prices for these services vary. LiveRamp can be found at https://www.liveramp.com/ and BlueKai can be found at https://www.oracle.com/marketingcloud/products/dmp/bluekai/.

It is important to note that while these advanced tools can be helpful in identifying and targeting specific audiences, they may also be more expensive and require a larger budget. It is up to you to decide which tools are the most appropriate and cost-effective for your needs.

2. Choose your platform: Decide where you want to run your campaign. Options include search engines like Google and Bing, and social media platforms like Facebook and Instagram.

Here are some examples of free tools and advanced tools for choosing the platform for your PPC (pay-per-click) campaign:

Free tools:

- Google Ads: https://ads.google.com/home/tools/keyword-planner/
- Bing Ads: https://ads.bingads.microsoft.com/home/tools/keyword-planner/
- Facebook Ads: https://www.facebook.com/business/tools/keyword-planner
- Instagram Ads: https://www.instagram.com/business/tools/keyword-planner/

Advanced tools:

- SEMrush: https://www.semrush.com/features/ad-platforms/
- Wordstream: https://www.wordstream.com/keywords
- AdEspresso: https://www.adespresso.com/
- Blukai: https://www.blukai.com/

These tools can help you choose the right platform for your PPC campaign by providing data on keyword trends, audience demographics, and other factors that can inform your decision. They may also offer additional features such as ad creation and campaign management, but these may require a paid subscription.

3. Choose your keywords: Select the keywords or phrases that you want to bid on, which will determine when your ad appears in search results or is shown to users.

Here is an example of how to choose keywords for a PPC campaign:

Imagine that you are the owner of a small bakery and you want to use PPC advertising to promote your business. You might start by brainstorming a list of relevant keywords, such as "bakery," "bread," "pastries," "cake," and "desserts." You can then use a free keyword research tool, such as Google's Keyword Planner, to help you identify additional keywords and phrases that are commonly searched for by users.

To use Google's Keyword Planner, simply enter your list of keywords and the tool will provide data on the monthly search volume for each keyword, as well as suggested bids for the keyword. You can use this information to help you choose the keywords that are most likely to drive traffic to your website and generate conversions.

Free keyword research tools:

- Google Keyword Planner: https://ads.google.com/home/tools/keyword-planner/
- Keywordtool.io: https://keywordtool.io/
- Answer the Public: https://answerthepublic.com/

Advanced keyword research tools:

- Ahrefs: https://ahrefs.com/

- SEMrush: https://www.semrush.com/
- KWFinder: https://www.kwfinder.com/

In addition to keyword research, you can also use tools like Google Ads and Bing Ads to manage your PPC campaigns. These platforms allow you to create and manage your ads, set your budget, and track the performance of your campaigns.

Google Ads: https://ads.google.com/ Bing Ads: https://www.bingads.microsoft.com/

Finally, there are also a number of advanced PPC management tools that can help you optimize your campaigns and improve your return on investment. Some examples include:

- Blukai: https://www.blukai.com/
- Opteo: https://opteo.com/
- AdEspresso: https://adespresso.com/
- Acquisio: https://www.acquisio.com/

By using these tools and following the steps outlined above, you can effectively choose the keywords for your PPC campaign and set up and manage your campaigns to reach your target audience and achieve your business goals.

4. Create your ad: Design an ad that will appeal to your target audience and effectively promote your product or service.

Here is an example of creating a PPC (pay-per-click) ad:

Imagine that you own a small bakery and want to create a PPC campaign to promote your new line of vegan pastries. You decide to run your campaign on Google Ads and have a budget of $500 per month.

First, you define your target audience as health-conscious individuals in your local area who are interested in vegan products.

Next, you choose your keywords, including "vegan pastries," "vegan bakery," and "vegan desserts." You bid on these keywords in order to have your ad appear when someone searches for these phrases on Google.

To create your ad, you write a compelling headline, such as "Indulge in Delicious Vegan Pastries from Our Bakery" and include a brief description of your products and a call to action, such as "Order Online Now." You also choose a relevant image to accompany your ad.

Finally, you set your budget and launch your campaign. Over the course of the month, your ad receives a total of 200 clicks and you spend a total of $400 on your campaign ($2 per click x 200 clicks = $400).

Free tools that can be helpful in creating PPC ads:

- Google Ads: Google's advertising platform allows you to create and manage PPC campaigns on Google and its partner websites. https://ads.google.com/

- Canva: This design platform offers a range of templates and tools for creating professional-looking ads and other marketing materials. https://www.canva.com/

Advanced tools with a fee may offer additional features and capabilities, such as:

- AdEspresso: This platform offers a range of tools for managing and optimizing PPC campaigns on platforms like Google Ads and Facebook Ads. https://www.adespresso.com/

- Bluekai: This platform offers data and insights to help advertisers create targeted and effective PPC campaigns. https://www.bluekai.com/

- WordStream: This platform offers a range of tools for managing and optimizing PPC campaigns, including keyword research, ad creation, and performance analysis. https://www.wordstream.com/

5. Set your budget: Determine how much you are willing to spend on your campaign, either on a daily or monthly basis.

To set your budget for a PPC (pay-per-click) campaign using a free tool, follow these steps:

1. Go to the platform where you are running your PPC campaign, such as Google Ads (https://ads.google.com/) or Bing Ads (https://ads.microsoft.com/).

2. Sign in to your account and select the campaign that you want to set a budget for.
3. Click on the "Budget" tab and enter the amount that you want to spend on your campaign.
4. Choose whether you want to set a daily budget or a monthly budget.
5. Click "Save" to set your budget.

Free tools for setting a budget for a PPC campaign include:

- Google Ads: https://ads.google.com/
- Bing Ads: https://ads.microsoft.com/
- Facebook Ads: https://www.facebook.com/business/ads
- Instagram Ads: https://www.instagram.com/business/ads/

Advanced tools for setting and managing a budget for a PPC campaign include:

- AdEspresso: https://www.adespresso.com/
- AdWords Editor: https://www.google.com/intl/en_us/adwordseditor/
- Hootsuite Ads: https://www.hootsuite.com/products/ads
- Marin Software: https://www.marinsoftware.com/
- WordStream: https://www.wordstream.com/

Note: Some of these tools may have paid versions with additional features, but all offer free versions as well.

Here is an example of setting a budget for a PPC (pay-per-click) campaign using a free tool:

Let's say that a clothing retailer wants to set a budget for their PPC campaign on Google Ads. Here is how they might do it:

1. Go to the Google Ads website (https://ads.google.com/) and sign in to their account.
2. From the dashboard, they click on the campaign that they want to set a budget for.
3. In the "Budget" tab, they enter the amount that they want to spend on their campaign. In this case, let's say they want to spend $1,000 per month on their PPC campaign.
4. They choose to set a monthly budget, since they want to allocate a specific amount of money to their campaign each month.
5. They click "Save" to set their budget.

Now, their PPC campaign will run until their budget of $1,000 has been reached, at which point it will stop showing their ads. They can adjust their budget at any time by returning to the "Budget" tab and entering a new amount.

6. Launch your campaign: Once you have completed these steps, you can launch your campaign and start reaching your target audience.

To launch a PPC (pay-per-click) campaign using a free tool, follow these steps:

1. Sign up for an account with the platform you want to use, such as Google Ads (https://ads.google.com/).
2. Click on the "Create" button and select "New campaign."

3. Choose the type of campaign you want to create, such as a search or display campaign.
4. Set your target location, language, and other targeting options.
5. Select the keywords you want to bid on and set your bid amount for each keyword.
6. Create your ad by entering the headline, description, and display URL for your ad. You can also add additional features like sitelinks and callout extensions to make your ad more effective.
7. Review your ad and make any necessary changes.
8. Set your budget and choose your delivery method.
9. Click "Save and continue" to launch your campaign.

Your campaign will then go live, and your ad will be shown to users who meet your targeting criteria and search for the keywords you have selected

7. Monitor and optimize: It is important to regularly monitor the performance of your campaign and make adjustments as needed. This includes analyzing the data on clicks, conversions, and other metrics to identify areas for improvement. You may also want to adjust your budget or targeting to optimize your return on investment.

Here are some tips for monitoring and optimizing your campaign:

1. Set goals: Determine what you want to achieve with your campaign, such as increasing website traffic or generating leads. This will help you measure the success of your campaign and identify areas for improvement.

- **Free Tool**: Google Analytics (https://analytics.google.com/)
- **Advanced Tool:** Mixpanel (https://mixpanel.com/)

2. Track your performance: Use the analytics and reporting tools provided by your PPC platform to track key metrics such as clicks, conversions, cost per click (CPC), and return on investment (ROI).

   - **Free Tool:** Google Analytics (https://analytics.google.com/)
   - **Advanced Tool:** Omniture (https://www.adobe.com/analytics/web-analytics.html)

3. Analyze your data: Use the data you have collected to identify trends and patterns that may indicate areas for improvement. For example, if you are getting a high number of clicks but a low number of conversions, you may need to adjust your ad copy or targeting.

   - **Free Tool:** Google Analytics (https://analytics.google.com/)
   - **Advanced Tool:** Tableau (https://www.tableau.com/)

4. Make adjustments: Based on your analysis, make changes to your campaign as needed. This could include adjusting your budget, targeting, ad copy, or landing pages.

- **Free Tool:** : Google Ads (https://ads.google.com/)
- **Advanced Tool:** AdEspresso (https://www.adespresso.com/)

5. Test and optimize: Use A/B testing to experiment with different versions of your ad and see which performs best. This will help you optimize your campaign for the best possible results.

- **Free Tool**:Google Optimize (https://www.google.com/analytics/optimize/)
- **Advanced:Toll** Optimizely (https://www.optimizely.com/)

6. Repeat the process: Regularly monitor and analyze your campaign data to ensure that it is performing well and make adjustments as needed.

- **Free Tool:** Google Analytics (https://analytics.google.com/)
- **Advanced Tool:** Adobe Analytics (https://www.adobe.com/analytics/web-analytics.html)

Managing a PPC campaign can be complex, and it is often helpful to work with a professional agency or a platform like Google Ads to ensure that your campaign is set up and managed effectively

Tips for optimizing your ad copy, targeting, and budget

Here are some tips for optimizing your ad copy, targeting, and budget in a PPC (pay-per-click) campaign:

1. Ad copy:

    - Use a clear, concise message that speaks to your target audience and conveys the benefits of your product or service.
    - Include a call to action to encourage users to take a specific action, such as clicking on your ad or visiting your website.
    - Use strong headlines and descriptive subheadings to grab attention and convey your message quickly.
    - Test different versions of your ad copy to see which performs best.

2. Targeting:

    - Use specific, relevant keywords to reach the right audience.
    - Use negative keywords to exclude users who are not interested in your product or service.
    - Use location and demographic targeting to reach users in specific areas or with certain characteristics.
    - Use interests and behaviors to target users with specific interests or who have taken certain actions online.

3. Budget:

    - Set a budget that is appropriate for your goals and resources.

- Monitor your budget closely and adjust as needed based on performance.
- Use bid adjustments to increase or decrease your bid amount for specific targeting options or locations.
- Use budget pacing to spread your budget out evenly over a specific time period.

By optimizing your ad copy, targeting, and budget, you can improve the performance of your PPC campaign and achieve your desired results.

8.Measuring and Analyzing Your SEO and SEM Results:

Importance of tracking and measuring your SEO and SEM efforts

Tracking and measuring your SEO (search engine optimization) and SEM (search engine marketing) efforts is important for several reasons:

1. Identify areas for improvement: By tracking and measuring your SEO and SEM efforts, you can identify areas where your website is performing well and areas where it could be improved. For example, you may discover that certain pages on your website have a high bounce rate, indicating that users are not finding the content relevant or engaging. By identifying these issues, you can take steps to improve the user experience and drive more qualified traffic to your website.

2. Monitor progress: Tracking and measuring your SEO and SEM efforts can help you monitor your progress

over time and see how your website is performing. This can help you understand the impact of your efforts and whether your strategies are effective. For example, you may see an increase in traffic or rankings after implementing a new SEO strategy or launching a new ad campaign.

3. Adjust your strategy: By analyzing your data, you can identify trends and patterns that may indicate the need to adjust your SEO and SEM strategies. For example, if you see a decline in traffic or rankings, you may need to make changes to your website or your marketing efforts. By regularly tracking and measuring your SEO and SEM efforts, you can stay up-to-date on the performance of your website and make necessary adjustments to stay ahead of the competition.

4. Maximize your return on investment: By tracking and measuring your SEO and SEM efforts, you can identify the most effective tactics and allocate your resources accordingly. This can help you maximize your return on investment and get the most value from your efforts. For example, if you see that a particular ad campaign is performing well, you may want to allocate more budget to that campaign and reduce your spending on other tactics that are not producing as good of results.

Overall, tracking and measuring your SEO and SEM efforts is essential to ensure that your website is performing well and achieving your desired results. It can help you identify areas for improvement, monitor your progress, adjust your strategy, and maximize your return on investment.

Tools and techniques for analyzing your website traffic and search engine rankings

There are several tools and techniques that can be used to analyze website traffic and search engine rankings, including both free and advanced options. These tools and techniques can be helpful for understanding how users are interacting with your website and identifying any issues or areas for improvement.

Some common tools and techniques for analyzing website traffic and search engine rankings include:

1. Google Analytics: This free tool from Google provides detailed insights into website traffic, including information on user demographics, behavior, and conversions.
2. Google Search Console: This free tool from Google allows you to monitor your website's performance on Google search and identify any issues with indexing or crawling.
3. Bing Webmaster Tools: This free tool from Bing allows you to monitor your website's performance on Bing search and identify any issues with indexing or crawling.
4. Ahrefs: This advanced tool offers a wide range of features for analyzing website traffic and search engine rankings, including keyword research, competitor analysis, and link building.
5. SEMrush: This advanced tool offers a range of features for analyzing website traffic and search engine rankings, including keyword research, competitor analysis, and link building.
6. Moz: This advanced tool offers a range of features for analyzing website traffic and search engine rankings,

including keyword research, competitor analysis, and link building.

In addition to using tools, there are also several techniques that can be used to analyze website traffic and search engine rankings. These include:

- Analyzing website logs: Examining log files from your website can provide valuable insights into how users are interacting with your site, including which pages are being visited and how long users are staying on each page.
- Conducting user surveys: Asking users for feedback on their experience with your website can help you identify any issues or areas for improvement.
- Analyzing site metrics: Examining metrics such as bounce rate, time on site, and conversion rate can provide valuable insights into how well your website is performing.
- Analyzing search engine rankings: Monitoring your rankings on search engines can help you identify any issues with your website's visibility and identify opportunities to improve your ranking.

Here is a list of tools and techniques for analyzing website traffic and search engine rankings, along with free and advanced providers:

Free tools for analyzing website traffic and search engine rankings:

- Google Analytics: https://www.google.com/analytics/ (free)

- Google Search Console: https://search.google.com/search-console/ (free)
- Bing Webmaster Tools: https://www.bing.com/toolbox/webmaster (free)

Advanced tools for analyzing website traffic and search engine rankings:

- Ahrefs: https://ahrefs.com/ (paid)
- SEMrush: https://www.semrush.com/ (paid)
- Moz: https://moz.com/ (paid)

Overall, there are a wide range of tools and techniques available for analyzing website traffic and search engine rankings, and the best option will depend on your specific needs and goals.

Best practices for using data to inform and improve your SEO and SEM strategies

Here are ten different strategies for using data to inform and improve your SEO (search engine optimization) and SEM (search engine marketing) efforts:

1. Keyword optimization: Use data from tools like Google Analytics and Google Search Console to identify which keywords are driving traffic to your website. Analyze the performance of these keywords and use them to optimize your website's content and structure to improve your rankings.

2. Ad testing: Use A/B testing or other types of experiments to test different versions of your ads and see which ones are most effective. Analyze the results of these tests and use them to optimize your ad copy, targeting, and budget.

3. User behavior analysis: Use tools like Google Analytics to analyze the behavior of users on your website. Look for trends or patterns in the data and use them to optimize your website's content and structure to improve the user experience and drive more conversions.

4. Content optimization: Use data to identify which types of content are most popular with your audience and use this information to create more of the same types of content or to optimize existing content to improve its performance.

5. Mobile optimization: Use data to understand how users are accessing your website on mobile devices and optimize your website for mobile to improve the user experience and drive more traffic.

6. Link building: Use data from tools like Ahrefs or Moz to analyze the quality and quantity of your website's backlinks and use this information to identify opportunities for building more high-quality links.

7. On-page SEO: Use data from tools like SEMrush or Ahrefs to analyze the on-page SEO of your website and identify any issues or opportunities for improvement.

8. Local SEO: Use data from tools like Google My Business and Yelp to understand how users are interacting with your business online and optimize your local SEO efforts to improve your visibility and drive more traffic.

9. Social media optimization: Use data from social media platforms like Facebook, Instagram, and Twitter to understand how users are interacting with your brand on social media and optimize your social media strategy to improve your engagement and reach.

10. Conversion optimization: Use data to understand how users are interacting with your website and identify any issues or opportunities for improving the conversion process. This could include analyzing the performance of different landing pages or testing different call-to-action buttons to see which ones are most effective.

By implementing these strategies and regularly analyzing and adjusting your efforts based on data, you can improve your SEO and SEM results and drive more traffic and conversions to your website.

9. Advanced SEO and SEM Strategies:

Tips for staying up-to-date with the latest SEO and SEM trends and best practices

Here are some tips for staying up-to-date with the latest SEO (search engine optimization) and SEM (search engine marketing) trends and best practices:

1. Follow industry blogs and publications: There are many blogs and publications that cover the latest SEO and SEM trends and best practices, such as Search Engine Land, Moz, and Search Engine Journal. Follow these resources to stay informed about the latest developments in the field.

Here are twenty advanced best web links for following industry blogs and publications:

- Search Engine Land: https://searchengineland.com/
- Moz: https://moz.com/blog
- Search Engine Journal: https://www.searchenginejournal.com/
- The SEM Post: https://www.sempost.com/
- Search Engine Watch: https://searchenginewatch.com/
- Search Engine Roundtable: https://www.seroundtable.com/
- Search Engine Land's Daily Search Forum Recap: https://searchengineland.com/the-daily-search-forum-recap-154587
- Search Engine Journal's SEO Blog: https://www.searchenginejournal.com/seo-blog/
- SEOmoz: https://moz.com/blog/category/search-engine-optimization
- Search Engine Land's SEO Blog: https://searchengineland.com/guide/seo
- The SEMrush Blog: https://www.semrush.com/blog/
- The Search Engine Roundtable Blog: https://www.seroundtable.com/blog
- The SEO Geeks Blog: https://www.seogeeks.com/blog/
- The Search Engine Guy Blog: https://www.thesearchengineguy.com/
- The Matt Cutts Blog: https://www.mattcutts.com/blog/

- The Search Engine Guys Blog: https://www.searchengineguys.com/blog/
- The Search Engine Guide Blog: https://www.searchengineguide.com/searchengineguide/blog/
- The SEO Blog: https://www.theseoblog.com/
- The Webmaster Blog: https://www.thewebmasterblog.com/
- The SEO Chick Blog: https://www.theseochick.com/blog/

By following these industry blogs and publications, you can stay up-to-date on the latest SEO and SEM trends and best practices.

2. Attend conferences and events: Attending conferences and events that focus on SEO and SEM can be a great way to learn from industry experts and stay up-to-date on the latest trends and best practices.

Here are twenty advanced best weblinks for attending conferences and events that focus on SEO (search engine optimization) and SEM (search engine marketing):

- MozCon: https://moz.com/mozcon
- SearchLove: https://www.distilled.net/searchlove/
- SMX (Search Marketing Expo): https://searchmarketingexpo.com/
- ClickZ Live: https://www.clickzlive.com/
- Pubcon: https://www.pubcon.com/
- BrightonSEO: https://www.brightonseo.com/
- SMX Advanced: https://www.smxadvanced.com/

- The Search Summit: https://www.thesearchenginesummit.com/
- HERO Conf: https://www.heroconf.com/
- LocalU Advanced: https://www.localu.org/events/
- SearchFest: https://www.portlandseo.org/searchfest/
- Digital Summit: https://www.digitalsummit.com/
- Search Engine Land's Search Marketing Expo: https://searchengineland.com/seo-events
- Inbound: https://www.inbound.com/
- Content Marketing World: https://www.contentmarketingworld.com/
- Search Marketing Expo West: https://searchengineland.com/seo-events
- SES (Search Engine Strategies): https://searchenginestrategies.com/
- Digital Summit Dallas: https://www.digitalsummit.com/dallas/
- Digital Summit Phoenix: https://www.digitalsummit.com/phoenix/
- Digital Summit Denver: https://www.digitalsummit.com/denver/

These conferences and events cover a wide range of topics related to SEO and SEM and offer opportunities to learn from industry experts, network with other professionals, and stay up-to-date on the latest trends and best practices.

3. Join online communities: There are many online communities, such as forums and LinkedIn groups, where SEO and SEM professionals discuss the latest trends and best practices. Joining these communities

can be a great way to stay informed and connect with others in the field.

Here are twenty advanced online communities that SEO and SEM professionals may find useful for staying informed and connecting with others in the field:

- Google's Webmaster Central Help Forum: https://www.google.com/webmasters/community/
- Moz's Q&A Forum: https://moz.com/community/q
- Reddit's /r/SEO subreddit: https://www.reddit.com/r/SEO/
- LinkedIn's SEO & SEM Professionals Group: https://www.linkedin.com/
- Search Engine Land's Search Marketing Forum: https://www.search engine land.com/smf/
- Warrior Forum's Search Engine Optimization section: https://www.warriorforum.com/search-engine-optimization/
- SEMrush's Expert Hub: https://www.semrush.com/expert-hub/
- Digital Marketing Institute's Community Forum: https://community.digitalmarketinginstitute.com/
- Bruce Clay's SEO Forum: https://www.bruceclay.com/seo/forum/
- Google's Google My Business Community: https://www.en.google.com/business/community/
- Internet Marketing Ninjas Forum: https://www.internetmarketingninjas.com/forum/
- Local SEO Guide's Local SEO Forum: https://www.localseoguide.com/local-seo-forum/
- SEO Chat's SEO Forum: https://www.seochat.com/forum/

- SEOmoz's Q&A Forum: https://www.seomoz.org/q/
- SEObook's SEO Forum: https://www.seobook.com/forum/
- Search Engine Roundtable's Forum: https://www.seroundtable.com/forum/
- SERPs' SEO Forum: https://www.serps.com/community/seo-forum/
- The Hoth's SEO Forum: https://www.thehoth.com/forum/
- Webmaster World's SEO Forum: https://www.webmasterworld.com/forum

4. Conduct your own research: Don't be afraid to do your own research and experimentation to stay up-to-date on the latest trends and best practices. Use tools like Google Analytics and Google Search Console to analyze your website's performance and test different strategies to see what works best.

There are many resources available online that can help you conduct research and stay up-to-date on the latest trends and best practices in web development. Some useful resources include:

- Google Analytics: This is a free tool offered by Google that allows you to track and analyze your website's traffic and performance. It provides a wealth of data and insights that can help you understand how visitors are interacting with your site and identify areas for improvement.
- Google Search Console: This is another free tool offered by Google that helps you monitor and maintain your website's presence in search results. It provides

information on search queries, clicks, and impressions, as well as alerts for any issues that may be affecting your site's performance.
- Moz: This is a company that provides a variety of tools and resources for SEO and digital marketing. They offer a range of products including the Moz Pro subscription service, which provides access to a range of advanced SEO and marketing tools, as well as educational resources and community support.
- Ahrefs: This is a company that provides a suite of tools for SEO and content marketing. Their tools include a keyword research tool, a backlink checker, and a site audit tool, among others. They also offer educational resources and a blog with articles on a range of topics related to SEO and digital marketing.
- SEMrush: This is a company that provides a range of tools and resources for SEO, PPC, and content marketing. They offer a subscription service that provides access to a suite of advanced tools and reports, as well as educational resources and a blog with articles on a range of topics related to digital marketing.

In addition to these resources, you can also find a wealth of information and guidance on web development and digital marketing through online communities and forums, such as Reddit's /r/webdev and /r/SEO subreddits, and Stack Overflow.

5. Follow thought leaders and experts: Follow thought leaders and experts in the SEO and SEM field on social media or through their blogs to stay informed about their latest insights and recommendations.

Here is a list of 20 experts in the field of SEO and SEM that you may want to follow to stay informed about the latest insights and recommendations:

- Rand Fishkin: Co-founder of Moz and author of the "Lost and Founder" podcast.
- Neil Patel: Founder of Crazy Egg, Hello Bar, and KISSmetrics, and a well-known blogger and speaker on digital marketing.
- Larry Kim: Founder of MobileMonkey and CEO of WordStream, and a frequent contributor to industry publications.
- Brian Dean: Founder of Backlinko, a leading SEO blog and resource.
- Danny Sullivan: Founding editor of Search Engine Land, a leading industry publication.
- Barry Schwartz: Founder of RustyBrick and a well-known blogger and speaker on SEO and digital marketing.
- Bill Slawski: Director of SEO Research at Go Fish Digital and a well-known blogger and speaker on SEO and digital marketing.
- Jennifer Slegg: Founder of The SEM Post, a leading industry blog, and a well-known speaker on SEO and digital marketing.
- John Mueller: Webmaster Trends Analyst at Google, and a frequent contributor to industry publications and conferences.
- Gary Illyes: Webmaster Trends Analyst at Google, and a frequent speaker at industry conferences.
- Duane Forrester: VP of Industry Insights at Yext, and a well-known speaker and blogger on SEO and digital marketing.

- Avinash Kaushik: Digital Marketing Evangelist at Google, and a well-known speaker and blogger on digital marketing.
- Aleyda Solis: Founder of Orainti, a digital marketing agency, and a well-known speaker and blogger on SEO and digital marketing.
- Matt Cutts: Former head of the web spam team at Google, and a well-known speaker and blogger on SEO and digital marketing.
- Eric Enge: CEO of Stone Temple Consulting, and a well-known speaker and blogger on SEO and digital marketing.
- Danny Dover: Co-founder of Blitz Metrics, and a well-known speaker and blogger on SEO and digital marketing.
- Marie Haynes: Founder of Marie Haynes Consulting, and a well-known speaker and blogger on SEO and digital marketing.
- Bruce Clay: Founder of Bruce Clay, Inc., and a well-known speaker and blogger on SEO and digital marketing.
- Jill Whalen: CEO of High Rankings, and a well-known speaker and blogger on SEO and digital marketing.
- Lisa Barone: CMO of Overit, and a well-known speaker and blogger on digital marketing.

By following these tips and staying dedicated to continuously learning and improving, you can ensure that you are up-to-date with the latest SEO and SEM trends and best practices.

Strategies for building and maintaining a long-term SEO and SEM plan

Here are 10 strategies for building and maintaining a long-term SEO and SEM plan, along with examples of each strategy and some tools that can help you implement them:

1. Keyword research: Identifying the keywords and phrases that your target audience is using to search for products or services like yours can help you optimize your website and content for those terms, increasing the likelihood that you will rank well in search results. Tools like Google's Keyword Planner, Ahrefs' Keywords Explorer, and SEMrush's Keyword Research tool can help you identify relevant keywords and phrases and get data on their search volume and competitiveness.

2. On-page optimization: Ensuring that your website is optimized for search engines involves a range of technical and content-related factors. Tools like Google's PageSpeed Insights and Lighthouse, Ahrefs' Site Audit tool, and SEMrush's On-Page SEO Checker can help you identify and fix technical issues on your website and ensure that your content is optimized for search engines.

3. Off-page optimization: Building high-quality backlinks from other reputable websites can help improve your website's visibility and authority in search results. Tools like Ahrefs' Backlink Checker and SEMrush's Backlink Audit tool can help you track and analyze the backlinks pointing to your website, and identify opportunities for earning more high-quality links.

4. Content marketing: Creating and distributing valuable, relevant, and consistent content can help attract and retain a clearly defined audience, and ultimately drive profitable customer action. Tools like CoSchedule's Headline Analyzer and SEMrush's Content Marketing Toolkit can help you create compelling headlines and optimize your content for search engines.

5. Social media marketing: Building and engaging with an audience on social media platforms can help drive traffic to your website and increase your visibility in search results. Tools like Hootsuite, Buffer, and Sprout Social can help you manage and schedule your social media posts and track their performance.

6. Paid search advertising: Running paid search ads through platforms like Google Ads can help you reach targeted audiences and drive traffic to your website. The Google Ads platform provides a range of tools and resources to help you set up and manage your paid search campaigns.

7. Email marketing: Sending targeted and personalized emails to your email list can help drive traffic to your website and nurture leads. Tools like Mailchimp and Constant Contact can help you manage and automate your email marketing campaigns.

8. Influencer marketing: Partnering with influencers or industry thought leaders can help expose your brand to a larger audience and earn backlinks to your website. Tools like BrandSnob and Upfluence can help you identify and connect with influencers in your industry.

9. Local SEO: Optimizing your website and online presence for local search can help improve your visibility and drive traffic from people searching for businesses in your area. Tools like Google My Business and Moz Local can help you optimize your local listings and ensure that your business information is accurate and consistent across the web.

10. Mobile optimization: Ensuring that your website is mobile-friendly and easy to use on smartphones and tablets is increasingly important, as more and more people are using mobile devices to access the web. Tools like Google's Mobile-Friendly Test and Ahrefs' Mobile Usability report can help you identify and fix any issues with your website's mobile experience.

10. Conclusion:

Recap of the main principles and techniques of SEO and SEM

In conclusion, SEO and SEM are crucial for businesses and organizations looking to improve their online visibility and drive targeted traffic to their websites. These strategies involve a range of principles and techniques that are designed to optimize and promote a website in order to improve its ranking in search results and attract qualified traffic.

Some of the main principles and techniques of SEO and SEM include keyword research, on-page optimization, off-page optimization, local SEO, technical SEO, and paid search advertising. By implementing these strategies in a strategic and cohesive manner, businesses can improve their ranking in search results, attract targeted traffic to their websites, and ultimately achieve their business goals.

It is important to note that SEO and SEM are ongoing efforts, and it is crucial to continuously monitor and optimize your strategies in order to achieve the best results. This may involve conducting your own research and experimentation, following thought leaders and experts in the field, and utilizing a range of tools and resources to analyze and optimize your website's performance. By investing in ongoing learning and optimization, you can ensure that your SEO and SEM efforts are effective and aligned with your business goals, and that you are able to adapt and evolve as the industry changes.

Importance of ongoing learning and optimization for successful SEO and SEM

Successful SEO and SEM require a commitment to ongoing learning and optimization. In today's digital landscape, it is important to constantly educate yourself on the latest trends and best practices, and to be proactive in testing and refining your strategies. This may involve conducting your own research and experimentation, following thought leaders and experts in the field, and utilizing a range of tools and resources to analyze and optimize your website's performance.

By investing in ongoing learning and optimization, you can ensure that your SEO and SEM efforts are effective and aligned with your business goals, and that you are able to adapt and evolve as the industry changes. Ignoring the importance of ongoing learning and optimization can lead to stagnation and a decline in your website's performance, making it more difficult to achieve your business objectives.

In summary, ongoing learning and optimization are critical for successful SEO and SEM. By staying up-to-date with the latest trends and best practices, and actively seeking out opportunities to improve and optimize your strategies, you can ensure that your website is able to compete and thrive in today's digital landscape.

Future outlook for the field of SEO and SEM.

The field of SEO and SEM is constantly evolving, and it is difficult to predict exactly what the future holds. However, there are a few key trends and developments that are likely to shape the field in the coming years:

1. Increased emphasis on user experience: As search engines continue to prioritize user satisfaction, businesses will need to focus on delivering high-quality and user-friendly experiences on their websites. This may involve things like improving the loading speed and mobile-friendliness of their websites, and prioritizing content that is valuable, relevant, and easy to understand.

2. Continued growth of voice search: As more and more people use voice assistants like Siri and Alexa to search the web, it will become increasingly important for businesses to optimize their websites and content for voice search. This may involve using long-tail keywords and structured data to make it easier for voice assistants to understand and interpret your content.

3. Greater importance of local SEO: With the proliferation of mobile devices, more and more people are using search engines to find local businesses and services. As a result, local SEO is likely to become even more important in the coming years, and businesses will need to optimize their websites and online presence for local search results in order to attract customers from their area.

4. Increased use of artificial intelligence and machine learning: As search engines continue to incorporate artificial intelligence and machine learning into their algorithms, it is likely that these technologies will play an increasingly important role in SEO and SEM. This may involve things like using AI to optimize website content and ad copy or using machine learning to improve targeting and budget allocation in paid search campaigns.

5. Greater emphasis on privacy and data protection: As concerns about privacy and data protection continue to grow, search engines and advertisers are likely to place an increased emphasis on respecting users' privacy and protecting their data. This may involve things like implementing stricter data protection policies and giving users more control over their personal data.

Overall, the field of SEO and SEM is likely to continue to evolve and change in the coming years, and businesses will need to stay up-to-date with the latest trends and best practices in order to remain competitive and achieve their business goals.

www.ingramcontent.com/pod-product-compliance
Lightning Source LLC
Chambersburg PA
CBHW052359220526
45465CB00003BB/1174